Jennifer Lopez

Jennifer Lopez

By
Kathleen Tracy

ECW *Press*

The publication of *Jennifer Lopez* has been generously supported
by the Government of Canada through the
Book Publishing Industry Development Program.

CANADIAN CATALOGUING IN PUBLICATION DATA
Tracy, Kathleen
Jennifer Lopez
ISBN 1-55022-419-0
1. Lopez, Jennifer, 1970- . 2. Actors - United States - Biography.
3. Singers - United States - Biography. I. Title.
PN2287.L66T72 2000   791.43'028'092   C00-931714-7

Front cover photo by The Work Group / Shooting Star.
Back cover photo by Barry King / Shooting Star.
Cover and interior design by Guylaine Régimbald.
Typesetting by Yolande Martel.
This book is set in Sari and Empire.

Printed by Printcrafters, Inc., Winnipeg, Manitoba, Canada.

Distributed in Canada by General Distribution Services,
325 Humber College Blvd., Etobicoke, Ontario M9W 7C3.

Distributed in the United States by LPC Group,
1436 West Randolph St., Chicago, IL 60607, U.S.A.

Distributed in Europe by Turnaround Publisher Services, Unit 3,
Olympia Trading Estate, Coburg Road, Wood Green, London, N2Z 6T2.

Distributed in Australia and New Zealand by Wakefield Press,
17 Rundle Street (BOX 2266), Kent Town, South Australia 5071.

Published by ECW PRESS,
2120 Queen Street East, Suite 200,
Toronto, Ontario M4E 1E2.
ecwpress.com

PRINTED AND BOUND IN CANADA

Table of Contents

Introduction

Jennifer Lopez is the right kind of performer coming of age at just the right time. Riding a wave of interest in all things Latin, Lopez blazed into the spotlight when she starred in the film *Selena*. She played the singer who herself was poised for crossover stardom when she was tragically murdered. The role transformed the public perception of Lopez from just another struggling Latin actress into bona fide Hollywood star. Since then, she has starred in several films, and, more recently, she has turned her sights on the music world, releasing a CD that has enjoyed what many critics consider a surprising success.

As any Hollywood celebrity can tell you, the price of stardom is steep. Thanks to a brief marriage that was undermined by her rising profile and to her subsequent romance with rap impresario Sean "Puffy" Combs, Lopez has become a media magnet. Her every move is reported in breathless detail, in part because drama seems to follow her wherever she goes. But whether she is simply the victim of circumstance or the creator of her own personal soap opera is a puzzle that many in the industry are still trying to solve.

One thing is certain, however: Jennifer Lopez is going where no other openly Latin actress has gone before. While Rita Hayworth and Raquel Welch enjoyed their own brand of stardom — primarily of the sex-symbol kind — neither woman flaunted her Latin heritage. Each came onto the Hollywood scene during an era when social codes were very different; each was encouraged to cosmetically downplay her ethnicity and change her name to something more Anglo-friendly. Lopez never even considered hiding her heritage, and, as a result, she breaks new ground with each role she takes.

Over the course of her career, Jennifer Lopez has gone from playing more stereotypical Hollywood-style roles — such as Melinda Lopez on the television shows *Second Chances* and *Hotel Malibu* — to non-race-specific roles — such as a US marshal in the film *Out of Sight*. Whether this is because Hollywood is finally opening itself up to minority actors or because

Lopez and New York City firemen at the *Frequency* premiere, 2000

Lopez is just very good at knocking down barriers is up for debate. But it is clear that for the foreseeable future Jennifer Lopez will forge ahead into unexplored territory.

"If I could describe myself in a few words," she has said, "*strong* would be one of them. I know what I want, and I'm willing to go after it." Still, like many actresses who suddenly find themselves famous, she is probably finding that striking a balance between professional success and personal happiness is an enormous challenge. The question is, just how hard is Lopez willing to work to have it all — and keep it?

JENNIFER LOPEZ

Dancing out of the Bronx

To most people, "New York" means "Manhattan." But Manhattan, that bustling metropolitan nerve center, is only one of the five districts, called boroughs, that make up New York City. Until 1989, each of these boroughs — the other four being the Bronx, Brooklyn, Staten Island, and Queens — was a separate county. They were then incorporated to form New York City, but each has retained its own distinctive personality.

The Bronx, which is north of Queens and east of Manhattan, is a borough of contrasts. Around the turn of the last century, immigrant families fresh from Europe and others from the tenements of Manhattan's Lower East Side came to settle in the Bronx. They were entering a more stable, yet upwardly mobile, community. Two of New York's most elegant neighborhoods, tree-lined Riverdale and Fieldston, are located in the Bronx, and the borough boasts many parks, including the New York Botanical Garden and the Wildlife Conservation Society, otherwise known as the Bronx Zoo.

Then there is the South Bronx. Anyone who saw the 1981 movie *Fort Apache — The Bronx* was presented with an indelible visual image of urban blight. The film was a police drama set in the infamous South Bronx, and it was named for what local police officers called the Forty-First Precinct station on Simpson Street. The area was so rife with violence and crime that the Fort Apache police felt as if they'd been assigned to work behind enemy lines. Although the film was fiction, it planted an image of the South Bronx as an urban disaster area in the national consciousness.

By the 1970s, the descendents of the immigrants who had moved to the Bronx looking for a better life were fleeing the South Bronx for the suburbs, leaving behind the poorer element of the population and a series of ghost neighborhoods. The Morrisania and Mott Haven sections of the South Bronx were estimated to have lost 150,000 residents during the decade. As more people left, arsonists, gangs, and drug dealers took over — in 1975 alone there were over thirteen thousand fires set in one twelve-square-mile area. With the economic base of the area so badly eroded, the once-handsome neighborhoods degenerated into a giant ghetto.

During his term as president in the late 1970s, Jimmy Carter made an infamous visit to Charlotte Street in the Bronx. Camera crews accompanying the nation's chief executive broadcast shocking footage of a warlike zone — burned-out buildings, abandoned neighborhoods, roving gangs of dead-eyed youths patrolling the ravaged streets. The South Bronx, a disaster of national proportions, became synonymous with American inner-city blight in general and offered a clear demonstration of the phenomenon called "white flight," the large-scale exodus of white, middle-class families from cities to suburbs.

It was here, in the Castle Hill area of the South Bronx, that Jennifer Lopez was born, on July 24, 1970. While the problems of the area could not be exaggerated, the people who stayed and called it home viewed it from a different perspective. Frank Sinatra may have sung about Manhattan, "If I can make it there / I'll make it anywhere," but the denizens of the South Bronx considered survival in this hostile environment to be the true measure of success. As one area resident, Deborah Harris, noted, "The people that come from the South Bronx hold it as a badge of honor. It means they're tough."

That toughness and resiliency are at the very core of who Jennifer Lopez is, and those qualities have informed her life every step of the way. So, in order to understand her feistiness and individuality, one first has to understand the environment she grew up in.

Although both her parents had jobs, life was still tough. "We all lived in a small apartment that was cold in the winter and hot in the summer," she recalls matter-of-factly. "But hey, there was always rice and beans." Lopez claims that despite the impressions of those living on the outside and looking in at the South Bronx, it wasn't all as scary as it seemed. "They made this movie called *Fort Apache — The Bronx* and everybody thinks that's what the Bronx is really like, some kind of war zone or something," she complained to Martyn Palmer of *Total Film*. "It's just like any other

Destined to be a star

inner city. I grew up in what I consider to be a nice neighborhood and for me it was . . . well, it was normal."

However mean the streets were that lay outside the front door, the Lopez family home was a safe haven for Jennifer and her two sisters, Lynda and Leslie. Her parents, David and Guadalupe, both Puerto Rican immigrants, were practicing Catholics who made sure their children received a parochial-school education. Jennifer now says, "Although I went to church every Sunday, it wasn't until I was an adult that I realized how important it is to have a relationship with God."

The Lopez girls had a strong work ethic instilled in them: David is a computer specialist for a Manhattan insurance company, and Guadalupe worked as a monitor at Holy Family School, which Jennifer attended. Later,

Lopez and her father at the *Men in Black* Premiere, 1997

Lupe Lopez would go to night school to earn her degree, and she would eventually be hired as a kindergarten teacher at Holy Family. The industrious Lupe was also strict with her girls. She was intent on keeping them from falling in with a bad crowd.

As a result, says Jennifer, "I was a good kid. I was always hugging people. I was very close to my grandparents and I listened to my mother and didn't do bad things. I didn't curse and I didn't run around. I was never naughty, but I was a tomboy and very athletic. I'd always be running around and playing sports and stuff. I did gymnastics, competed nationally in track, and was on the school softball team."

Sports were a natural outlet for Jennifer's intense physical energy, but her real passion was performing. She recalls that Lupe "raised us on musicals. She would sit us in front of the television and I loved it." Although David and Lupe didn't know it, Jennifer was already fantasizing about being a star, a fantasy she immersed herself in whenever she took the long subway ride into Manhattan. "I just knew it was something I wanted to do." The type of performer she dreamed of becoming was a dancer. "I always wanted to sing and dance and be in movies," she explained to Brantley Bardin of *Details*, "but when you're little, you don't really understand what the 'rich and famous' part is all about — it's just a catchphrase that means 'I wanna be doing what they're doing up there.' And ever since I was three that's how I was — I always felt all this drama inside of me."

David and Lupe may not have considered performing to be a real career choice, but they did encourage their children to participate in a range of activities, hoping that this would help keep the girls out of trouble. So Jennifer was enrolled in the Ballet Hispanico.

"My mom took us to dance classes when we were young," Jennifer told *People* magazine. "My mother might have been a little bit of a frustrated actress, but she wasn't a stage mom. We went to dance classes every weekend. But it wasn't til I got older that I started to pursue it myself."

Close in age — Lynda is only two years younger than middle daughter Jennifer, who herself is just a year younger than Leslie — the three sisters would act out television series together at home. Their favorite was *Charlie's Angels*. "When we would play, I was always Jaclyn Smith," Lynda admitted to *People*. "Leslie was Kate Jackson. Jen was whoever the blonde was — Farrah or Cheryl Ladd."

Jennifer Lopez's mom
HENRY MCGEE / GLOBE PHOTOS

It's ironic that the woman who would later become a role model for ethnic girls everywhere had no role model herself when she was a child. "There weren't a lot of actresses I could identify with, being Puerto Rican," she pointed out to Julian Ives during a *Mr. Showbiz* interview. "There were zero Latinos on TV, so Rita Moreno was the only one I identified with." One result of having few, if any, Latin figures to identify with in the media, Lopez says, is that "If you don't see anybody like you there, it's like, 'Well, I guess I don't exist.'"

Lupe told Denis Duggan of *Newsday*, "I made my three daughters watch musical films like *West Side Story*. 'Sit and watch,' I told them, and they did." Jennifer herself remarks, "I loved *West Side Story*, and that says it all right there. I identified with it. It was my favorite movie and I wanted to be Rita Moreno. Not Maria: she was kind of wimpy and she blamed her brother for things."

Lopez says she watched *West Side Story* more than a hundred times as a kid. "I loved that it was a musical and about Puerto Ricans and that they were living where I lived. I wanted to be Anita because I love to dance and she was Bernardo's girlfriend and he was so hot. But then Maria was the star of the movie. So it was basically like, I gotta be Maria. I think that's the actress in me, wanting to be the center of attention and the star of the show. I just always wanted to achieve and be proud of myself."

Although she gravitated towards musicals because of the dancing, music of all kinds influenced Jennifer during her youth. Walking through her neighborhood she would hear a symphony of musical styles and genres. "I was in third grade when The Sugarhill Gang's 'Rapper's Delight' changed my life," she told Michael A. Gonzales of *Latina* magazine. "But then, when I came home, my mother would be listening to Celia Cruz, Tito Puente, or Diana Ross. That's my background. It's what I call Latin soul." Jennifer's sisters also responded to the music — Lynda is now a disc jockey and Leslie is a music teacher.

Although Jennifer was a self-described "good kid," she did learn how to handle herself out in the world. No amount of parental love could protect the Lopez sisters from the reality of the streets. Home life was one thing; school life was quite another. So Jennifer, the affectionate little girl who adored her grandparents, learned to stand up for herself when the situation called for it, such as one time in the fourth grade. "There were these two best friends and I started getting on with one of them," Jennifer explained to Anthony Noguera of *FHM*. "The other one got jealous, so she told me that the other girl was always talking about me. In the end, I confronted her; she denied it, so I pushed her in the face. We started fighting and I knocked her down. It was pretty ugly, and although I'm not proud of the event, I did win the fight. Nobody ever messed with me after that, and I graduated from school unscathed."

Even so, as Lopez is quick to point out, that was then and this is now. "I was nine. I'm not a violent person. Women hitting each other is low class, and it looks ridiculous and stupid. But I can, and would, defend myself if I had to. I'm not going down without a fight, that's for sure. I started that fight in fourth grade, but," she adds, "I've matured since then."

Although she would later become known as one of Hollywood's sul-

triest sex symbols, as a kid, she explains, "I wasn't one of the hotter girls
— my body hadn't developed much — but I was one of the cooler girls."
Along with her best friend since second grade, Arlene Rodriguez, Jennifer
dressed "very Bronx, hip-hop, boyish" in tight jeans and boots. "Then
Madonna came along," she says. "I always admired her, liked her music,
her sense of style. I like that she changed all the time."

When she was thirteen, Jennifer had a brush with death. "A truck carrying compressed gas cylinders hit my mom's car," she told Noguera. "The
only thing that saved my life was the fact that I was bending down tying my
shoes in the front seat, because his headlight flew through the windscreen
and ended up in the back of the car. It would have smashed my face in. I
don't even remember exactly how my nose got fractured, but that's why it
looks like it does. People always tell me I look like I was hit with a hammer,
but I like 'my nose. In profile it's good, but if you look straight at me or
touch it, you can see the flatness." That broken nose and the character it
gave her face ultimately just enhanced her blossoming looks.

Soon enough, this Latin beauty would begin to fascinate members of
the opposite sex. But Jennifer didn't date much as a kid, and she was never
interested in playing the field — she was strictly a one-boy kind of girl. In
grade school she developed her first crush. The object of her desire was a
boy named Charles, "who had blue eyes and black hair. He was so cute. I
never kissed him because I was only ten years old. He'd come over to my
house every day and my mom would give us sandwiches and milk. I dreamt
of marrying him. I saw him years later when he'd grown up, and let's put it
this way — he peaked early," she laughs.

When she was still very young, Jennifer began to develop the curves
for which she would later become famous. "I had a very voluptuous body
from the time I was eleven," she told Stephen Rebello of *Movieline*. "My
mother used to say, 'I'm so worried about Jennifer because she's so sexy.
I'm afraid she's going to get pregnant.' The taste in my neighborhood was
for voluptuous women, see? I knew guys liked me. Back then, in the third,
fourth grade, there were girls who already had tits and boyfriends, they
were always kissing in the school closet. Not me. I was more of a late
bloomer, like I didn't get into it until seventh grade, twelve years old."

In the tenth grade Lopez started dating her first real boyfriend, David
Cruz. "He made me feel like a hot babe," she says. "We started dating
when I was fifteen and dated only each other for nine years. We were very

careful. I'm not saying we weren't having sex, because we were," she ad-mits, revealing that she lost her virginity with David when she was seven-teen. But — despite her earlier daydreams about Charles — Jennifer was far more interested in pursuing a career than settling down.

"We lived in the same neighborhood and [David would] see me in, like, a weird hat, wearing something I'd cut together from a picture I'd seen in a magazine and I'd be just going to the track to run." David was special because he could appreciate that Jennifer, as she puts it, "was creating my own style. Everybody would look at me like I was a nerd — 'What is she doing? What is she wearing?' — because people didn't do that in my neigh-borhood; people didn't work out or take care of their bodies. If people see you striving for things, it threatens them. I was like, 'This two-bit town isn't big enough for me.'" David would simply say, "Jennifer has bigger plans." And if she was accused of being ambitious, Jennifer would shrug off the implied insult. "I've always said I was."

Although in her heart Jennifer dreamed of stardom and believed she could achieve whatever she put her mind to, she also had a practical side, and for a while she intended to get a license to be a hairstylist. Her first job was in a salon, sweeping up the hair from the floor. At home she would practice her styling techniques on her patient sisters. "It would look good at first," Jennifer recalls, "but then it would be really bad because I didn't know what the hell I was doing."

She had no lack of confidence, however, when it came to performing. In high school she participated in all the plays and continued taking dance classes. Even though Jennifer never hid her passion for dance, her parents still assumed that she would pursue a more solid profession — maybe she'd become a lawyer. "Where I come from, you got a job as a bank teller and got married, and being driven didn't mean wanting to be a star. It meant being a lawyer instead of a secretary." Although being an attorney "was aiming really high where I came from," says Lopez, "it was an attainable goal."

She did try to juggle her parents' hopes for her and her own aspira-tions, but she soon realized that she had to live her own life, whatever the consequences. Still, it was hard for her to tell her parents that she was dropping out of Baruch College in New York City after only one semester to devote herself to dancing. Their response was understandably less than enthusiastic.

Lopez's senior photo from Preston High School, 1987

Senior year

"It was a fight from the beginning," admits Lopez. "When I told my parents I wasn't going to college and law school, they thought it was really stupid to go off and try to be a movie star. No Latinas did that — it was just this stupid, foolish, crapshoot idea to my parents and to everybody who knew me."

Jennifer wasn't willing to let this lack of support deter her, but she was still faced with the problem of not knowing where to start. "I knew I wanted to perform as a career, although I didn't know how to go about it." So she decided to train hard and keep her eyes open for opportunities. Each day she'd take the number 6 subway train — which years later would be the inspiration for the title of her first album, *On the 6* — and travel to Manhattan, where she would train at different dance studios, studying ballet and jazz, while sniffing out auditions. "I was happy at the time, riding that train every day," Jennifer recalls. "To me, the struggle has always been the fun part." Soon she found herself living the exciting yet tenuous life of a "gypsy," the Broadway term for a professional dancer.

Devoting herself completely to dance often meant scraping by on very little money. "There were times when I was really down to my last dollar," she told Anthony Noguera. "And then my last fifty cents . . . and then my last quarter. I'd dance in a piece-of-garbage rap or pop video for fifty bucks and make the money last a whole month."

A turning point for Jennifer came after M.C. Hammer released his smash hit "You Can't Touch This." "All the auditions started becoming hip-hop auditions," she remembers. "I was good at it, and they were like, 'Ooh, a light-skinned girl who can do that. Great, let's hire her!'"

Soon Lopez was being hired to work on some high-profile music videos, such as Janet Jackson's "That's the Way Love Goes." Her foot firmly in the door, she went on to do a series of better dance jobs. She traveled to Japan to appear in the chorus of dancer, singer, and choreographer Hinton Battle's musical *Synchrocinicity*. She also toured Europe with the *Golden Musicals of Broadway* review as well as regional productions of *Oklahoma!* and *Jesus Christ, Superstar*. "You have to be so committed," Jennifer says of her early days as a dancer. "People say you need something just to fall back on; I don't believe in that."

Out of those adventures Lopez developed a moxie that at times helped her to fly by the seat of her inexperienced pants. She recalls her first commercial audition in 1989, for an Olympics promotion, during which the director asked her if she knew how to use a trampoline. Without hesitation, she assured him that she did — even though she had never been on one in her life. And, without hesitation, the director hired her.

As it turned out, the commercial was never broadcast, and perhaps it was just as well. "I sucked," Lopez says bluntly. The problem, she would later come to believe, was that commercial work was just too superficial for her. "You have to believe in something," she says, explaining why she stopped going out on commercial calls. She'd learned that when it came to being a mouthpiece for an advertiser she couldn't "be convincing."

Whatever financial gains she may have sacrificed by shunning commercial work Lopez would recoup in renewed focus and drive. Another quality that served her well at this time was her thick skin. "My older sister and I both started out in musical theater," Lopez told Stephen Rebello of *Movieline*. "She has a great voice and she had more of a chance of making it than I did. But she couldn't take the rejection. You have to get up there and say, 'You like me?' And if they say, 'No,' it's like, 'OK. Fuck you! Next? How about you? Do you like me? Or you? Or you?'"

On another occasion she put it like this: "If you're gonna make it in this business, you need the kind of personality that you have to do it or die, there's no alternative."

So, when Jennifer went to Los Angeles to test her wings as a performer, she considered it a matter of creative life and death.

Right Time, Right Place, Right Girl

"Dancing has always been my first love," Jennifer Lopez told *Talk* magazine interviewer Bob Morris. "Acting and singing are internal, but dancing is pure physical expression. For a long time, I didn't understand why a dancer would want to become an actor." Eventually she would.

In 1990, Fox put out a national casting call for dancers to work on a new comedy-sketch show, called *In Living Color*, which the television network was developing with Keenan Ivory Wayans. Along with thousands of other hopefuls, Lopez tried out for the job, going through a series of auditions, each one more nerve-wracking than the previous one, because with each callback the chances of getting the job increased significantly. When the final cut was made, Lopez, Lisa Marie Todd, and Michelle Whitney-Morrison were hired to be the show's "Fly Girls." Their contributions to the series would be choreographed by Rosie Perez. Lopez was about to take part in a project that would break color barriers, establishing a career pattern.

With some notable exceptions, since the early 1980s television has reflected a white, middle-class, suburban sensibility, particularly in its sitcoms. While network executives love to point to *The Cosby Show* as an example of their commitment to diversity, the Huxtables were no more representative of urban American life than Donna Reed's family had been in their time. What *In Living Color* did was bring urban hip-hop culture to the American heartland — without apology and often without any sense of political correctness. And it was an instant hit.

Like *Laugh-In* before it, with a hint of *The Carol Burnett Show* thrown in, *In Living Color* held very little sacred. It stretched the limits of the network censors with characters such as Handi-Man, a superhero with cerebral palsy; the Home Boys, a pair of con artists who chanted for "mo' money"; and Blaine and Antoine, a flamboyantly gay version of Siskel and Ebert. It even made a sly jab at Cosby with the Buttmans, a family with buttocks for foreheads.

Reveling in this weekly madness was the cast — a crop of newcomers, including several of Keenan's own brothers and sisters, some of whom would go on to attain individual success. Rosie Perez would segue from choreography to acting, later winning an Oscar nomination; David Alan Grier would star in a comedy series of his own and return to his theater roots by starring in a Broadway revival of *A Funny Thing Happened on the Way to the Forum*; Damon Wayans would find success as a television writer; and James Carrey would go on to become famous as Jim Carrey, one of the movie world's twenty-million-dollar men. "They were among the most talented people I've ever worked with," says former Fox president Peter Roth, who now heads up Warner Brothers Television. "They broke form and pushed content."

The sensibility and tone of the series was set by its creator, Keenan Ivory Wayans, who developed the idea shortly after the release of his blaxploitation film parody *I'm Gonna Get You Sucka*. Despite *In Living Color*'s obvious uniqueness — a sketch show with a multicultural cast — Wayans's point was never political. "Keenan was always looking for the bigger and broader joke," said a former writer on the show, Fox Bahr (who would later serve as an executive producer for another Fox sketch show, *Mad TV*, which had more than a few similarities to *In Living Color*). Speaking to Neal Justin of the *Minneapolis Star-Tribune*, Bahr recalled that "Keenan always wanted us to top ourselves — then get out."

Keenan's brother Damon told Justin, "We created characters that people don't come into contact with every day and helped people understand them. The good thing about sitcoms is, the characters stay true. You can take Archie Bunker and put him in a space shuttle and he's still going to be Archie Bunker. That's what we did." And another cast member, Kelly Coffield, added, "It wasn't so much what's funny this week as what's funny, period."

Because the show had so much sexual content, you might assume that the voluptuous Fly Girls constantly had to field suggestive comments

The *In Living Color* "Fly Girls" (Lopez at bottom right)

and overtures from hormonally charged male cast members. But Lopez says the production schedule solved that problem: "We were separated. We rehearsed in different rooms, and we only taped on one day when they weren't there. But we knew them and they were great to us. It was a good show . . . hip and cool."

As so often happens, the show almost became a victim of its own success. In the middle of the 1992–93 season, the network informed Keenan that it was going to air reruns of the show as a replacement for another series that had been canceled. Wayans objected, claiming that the extra exposure would hurt the syndication value of the show. But it wasn't Wayans's decision, and Fox aired the reruns in spite of his protests. Wayans was already unhappy with Fox because the Standards and Practices Office, otherwise known as the network censors, had begun to clamp down on the show after an *In Living Color* halftime special aired during the 1992 Super Bowl. In it, Blaine and Antoine reviewed the first half of the game while proclaiming their affection for the "tight ends" and suggesting that several of the players were gay. So, when Fox went ahead with its plan to broadcast the show twice a week, Wayans, along with all of his brothers and sisters, abruptly quit, even though the show was still in production. Although it finished out its third season and would go on for another year, the defections proved fatal, and *In Living Color* aired its last original episode in August of 1994.

While the demise of the series was a bitter blow to the Wayans clan, for Lopez it was a signal that it was time to close one door and walk through another. But, although she'd been strictly a background player, her *In Living Color* years were an invaluable learning experience that came with a steady paycheck. When those paychecks stopped coming Jennifer had to push forward. She had taken acting lessons while still working on the series to prepare herself for the speaking roles she was confident would follow.

Through *In Living Color* Jennifer found her first manager, Eric Gold. A coproducer of the series, Gold believed that Jennifer Lopez was a talent ready to explode. "There was just an unshakable confidence about Jennifer," Gold recalled to David Handleman of *Mirabella*. "No doubt, no fear. The girl just had it." Gold had almost as much confidence in Lopez's future as she did, and he would eventually leave producing behind to concentrate on launching the career of his extremely ambitious and dedicated new client.

Later, Gold would tell Bob Morris of *Talk* that Lopez "was always very determined. When she decided to try acting, I told her she'd have to lose weight. The very next day she had a trainer and was out jogging. She knew she had to or she'd be a fat girl." For Gold, *In Living Color* would prove to be a double gold mine — he also took Jim Carrey under his wing, and the rest is history.

Jennifer was less concerned about money than about opportunity, and her work ethic paid off almost immediately. She appeared in the otherwise forgettable television movie *Nurses on the Line: The Crash of Flight 7*, starring Lyndsay Wagner. Lopez was one of a group of student nurses whose plane crashes in the Mexican jungle. Then, even before *In Living Color* had wrapped, she was offered a role in another series.

In Hollywood, jobs often come through personal channels. It's all about who you know. In this case, a member of *In Living Color*'s production team was married to a producer/writer who was working on a new drama for Fox and suggested that he audition Jennifer Lopez for a part. He did, and Jennifer was eventually hired as the recurring character of Lucy on the series *South Central*. It was one of the first serious attempts by a network to launch a black "dramedy." Created by Michael J. Weithorn and Ralph Farquhar, who had worked on *Family Ties* and *Married . . . with Children*, respectively, the story revolved around a divorcée, played by Tina Lifford, who loses her job and goes to work as an assistant manager of a food co-op.

Starring in the series as Lifford's son, Andre, was Larenz Tate, who had just made a huge cinematic splash with his stunning performance as a sociopathic sixteen-year-old killer in *Menace II Society*. His character kills two liquor-store owners in the opening minutes of that movie then considers selling the videotape of the murders to exploit its entertainment value. Tate's performance was so strong that many assumed he was a kid from the streets. Hollywood insiders knew he was actually a terrific young actor with a varied résumé that listed a role on the CBS sitcom *The Royal Family* opposite Redd Foxx. Ralph Farquhar described Tate as "probably one of the leading young actors in the country right now."

Tate's success in *Menace II Society* helped *South Central* to generate a lot of buzz prior to its debut, although by the time the show aired the buzz had turned to scrutiny. Setting a series in L.A.'s notorious South Central district was risky enough; occasionally playing it for laughs seemed like creative suicide. Critics, however, were willing to give the show some breathing room, even if they sometimes seemed bemused. *Newsday* noted, "*South Central* zooms into one pressure-cooker household, where an abandoned wife (Tina Lifford) tries to ride herd on her two kids — a too-cool high school boy (Larenz Tate) and his put-upon sister (Tasha Scott) — along with a young foster child (Keith Mbulo) whose unchangingly blank countenance already reflects a scarred life. Lifford's character has just lost her job; she fears she's losing her son to the streets; she's already lost too many of the important men in her life, and she's wondering whether her sanity is the next element [to go] out the door. The folks here know laughing about it ain't gonna make it better. But they laugh anyway. And they ask us to, too."

While some may have thought it was in poor taste to find humor in despair and social inequity, Farquhar disagreed: "The whole idea for *South Central* is to really explore the multi-camera format, to get outside those parameters TV has been using since *I Love Lucy*. So we decided to do hand-held stuff. You know, let's experiment a little bit. And with that, the audience is not sure what to expect when they watch the show. They hear laughter, and they think, 'What's going on here?' Then there's a dramatic turn, and, 'Hmm, usually when I'm watching a show like this it's all light and fun.'" Farquhar then added, "What I think we've managed to accomplish is that drama and comedy occupy the same space. One doesn't end where the other begins. There's comedy within the dramatic moments, or drama within the comedy."

Fox was willing to give Farquhar a chance to do the show his way, unlike CBS, which had originally developed the series but backed out when it didn't seem funny enough. Rose Catherine Pinkney, the former director of programming for Twentieth Century Fox Television, called it "a realistic but positive depiction of life in the nineties" and went on to say, "If you're expecting *ha, ha, ha* every two minutes, you're not going to enjoy this show. But if you want honest laughs from an honest family when it's right, then you'll like it."

When *South Central* premiered in April 1994, many viewers found it neither funny nor easy to follow. One of Farquhar's other ideas was to present a true slice of life, a series in which characters suddenly appear without introduction and the story is nonlinear. "There's enough TV that tells you everything three times, just so you can get it," the producer complained. "On this, we were more concerned with the emotion of it. That leaves a lot sometimes to one's imagination. But there's a lot of debate that comes as a result of viewing TV this way."

And, as it turned out, a lot of confusion. Results of audience testing conducted by the network showed that women accepted the plot holes and the haphazard story development, while men were solidly turned off by Farquhar's nontraditional approach. Yet it was the show's content that generated the most controversy. In one episode, the characters humorously debate the merits of being called "African American" as opposed to "black."

"We're going to touch all sides," said Farquhar, who himself is a product of Chicago's equally notorious South Side. "You know, TV tends to be stacked. We're going to dare to be politically incorrect, if that suits the characters' points of view. The show takes a basically neutral position."

For all the good intentions of Fox and Farquhar, *South Central* was doomed to fail. Although the networks had been criticized for their lack of multicultural programming, the series came under fire almost immediately from an unexpected source: the black community, the very constituency *South Central*'s producers had sought to represent. At issue was the charge that the show promoted racial stereotypes.

Actress Marianne Aalda-Gedeon of the show *The Royal Family* complained to journalist Ray Richmond, "Basically they're saying that a show about an unemployed woman who's been deserted by her husband to raise three foul-mouthed, disrespectful, beeper-carrying, front-yard-urinating kids is as good as it gets? And I'm supposed to like it? I don't think so. I mean, this mother, with the way she is, would not have raised children who acted like this. I know this because I don't allow that behavior in my home, and neither does any other African American mother I know."

Even Bill Cosby joined the fray. Speaking during his induction into the Academy of Television Arts and Sciences Hall of Fame, he dropped his funnyman persona to chastise the television industry: "Stop this horrible massacre of images that are being put on the screen now, I'm begging you, because it isn't us."

Farquhar defended his show by calling it "too realistic," and accusing its detractors of wanting "us as a show to deny the existence of single black mothers, teenage boys who struggle with the sometimes darker elements of the neighborhoods where they live, and . . . bab[ies] born addicted to crack."

For the second time during her still-fledgling career, Lopez found herself associated with a project that not only pushed the creative envelope within Hollywood's entertainment community but also pushed the social buttons of the TV audience. For her, however, the brouhaha was secondary to the excitement of having her first real acting job. She was glad the show was generating such interest and hoped it would last long enough for her to gain valuable on-the-job experience.

While *South Central* may have broken new ground, the series was on shaky terrain from the start, and for all the talk of presenting the audience with something different, the bottom line is that not enough people tuned in to warrant keeping the show on the air past August 1994. In fact, that same spring and summer Fox canceled not only *South Central* but also *Roc* and *Sinbad*, two other high-quality programs developed to reflect an African American sensibility. In one fell swoop, nearly all the shows with minority casts were wiped out. And the reaction was passionate.

Angry *Roc* star Charles Dutton sounded off during an interview. His show, he proclaimed, was a victim of a new racial segregation. The rule had become, "No blacks, Latins or dogs need apply after 9 P.M." — the time network programmers generally reserve for their serious dramas. Critics were equally concerned about the trend. Columnist Clarence Page of the *St. Louis Post-Dispatch* wrote, "Imagine, for a moment, the public outcry if the networks were to announce that, in the new fall season, *Blossom* and *Married . . . with Children* would be the only prime-time network television programs that would portray the lives of white people in America. Right. It couldn't happen. Audiences would not tolerate such a narrow portrayal of white people. The public would demand more diversity — more dramas, more docu-dramas, more action, more soaps, more stories of love, more stories of hate, more triumph, more tragedy, more of a reflection of real life as we know it."

Page singled out *Blossom* and *Married . . . with Children* because those sitcoms had the distinction of being the only two predominantly white programs that — according to a Madison Avenue survey of black and white viewing habits — made it into the top-ten list of black viewers' favorites. "In other words," Page concluded, "blacks, like whites, love to see whites cavort in situation comedies. That's OK. The marketplace works best when it offers choices. Comedy thrives on stereotypes. But life thrives on variety. In the absence of any other images, stereotypes become a form of real-life tragedy."

Another, largely unspoken concern, was that because there were so few roles for minorities on prime-time television, the cancellation of these three shows had put a lot of talented minority actors out of work. Many of them would have trouble finding new jobs. For every Will Smith there are a hundred Clifton Powells — the actor who played the co-op boss on *South Central*. Jennifer Lopez, however, was not destined to wind up unemployed. Even though *South Central* went off the air after only a couple of months, its run was long enough to give her the necessary exposure. She had caught the eye of those Hollywood executives who were looking to add minorities of any shade to their casts in an effort to ward off the intensifying criticism of coalitions and critics alike.

For Jennifer, it would truly be a case of being in the right profession at just the right time in Hollywood history. The entertainment community seemed suddenly willing to consider the possibility that a leading lady didn't have to be a blue-eyed blond from Nebraska; that a name with an ethnic ring wasn't box-office or ratings anathema; that a modern-day sex symbol didn't have to look as if she were suffering from some eating disorder.

Anyone who insisted on clinging to the stereotypical Hollywood conception of beauty was about to get burned by Jennifer Lopez's star vapor trail. She was rising fast.

First and Second Chances

The time had come. Jennifer Lopez would get to demonstrate her dramatic-acting chops in a new CBS series called *Second Chances*. The show was set in the fictional seaside town of Santa Rita, California, and it starred Connie Sellecca, who had costarred in two previous hit series, *The Greatest American Hero* and *Hotel*. Prior to the show's debut, in a display of Hollywood image consciousness, Sellecca's publicist sent out a press alert to the effect that Connie had "cut off her trademark long hair" for *Second Chances* — so, "*Please* destroy the long-haired photographs you have on file."

For Sellecca, the series was the best of both worlds: she had steady work, but, because the show had a large cast, she also had time for her family — unlike the other hour series she had worked on, *Second Chances* filmed five days a week instead of six. She had recently married *Entertainment Tonight* anchor John Tesh, and she had a son, Gib, from her previous marriage to actor Gil Gerard. "I was asked in an interview how it felt to be in an ensemble cast in *Second Chances*," Sellecca said. "I'm enjoying the situation. I can sit back and enjoy some of the younger actors and actresses, remembering what I was like and realizing I'm not that way anymore."

The series, categorized as a "serial drama/romantic mystery," was created by Lynn Marie Latham and Bernard Lechowick, the husband-and-wife team behind the critically acclaimed World War II family drama *Homefront*, which ABC had scrapped before its time. *Second Chances* had been bought by CBS on the strength of a two-hour script written by Latham and Lechowick, who had also done time on *Knot's Landing*. Explained

Latham, "They said, 'We know what you do, we love what you do, do it again for us.'"

Although not as cinematic as *Homefront*, *Second Chances* was another well-written drama, and it proved to be more accessible to a broader audience. The ensemble drama also starred Matt Salinger, Ronny Cox, Michelle Phillips, Megan Follows, and Justin Lazard — Jennifer's love interest.

The two-hour pilot was engrossing, and it generated solid ratings. Santa Rita is introduced as a decent, if not perfect, place to raise a family. Although most of the citizens are socially tolerant and the crime rate is low, the town cannot escape the type of problems that plague communities nationwide — such as racism and murder. Sellecca played Dianne Benedict, a public defender with aspirations to become a judge and the single mother of an eight-year-old boy. Megan Follows costarred as Dianne's sister, Kate, a woman with a penchant for picking the wrong man. Jennifer portrayed waitress Melinda Lopez. Melinda marries Kevin Cook, a law student whose wealthy parents turn out to be racists. Needless to say, the honeymoon is short-lived. As the show revolved around these three women, it meant that for the first time Lopez was appearing in a legitimate costarring role.

Second Chances was the kind of series that critics have a love-hate relationship with: they love a show because it's good; they get hooked; then they hate it when it gets yanked, as most critically acclaimed shows do. Marvin Kitman of *Newsday* lamented, "I am tired of getting involved in good shows, and then recommending them to readers who similarly get involved, only to see them disappear into the land of the living dead (hiatus) or worse. It's a particularly relevant concern because *Second Chances* is on CBS, whose commitment to new programs this season is not as intense as it might be. . . . Will *Second Chances* get a second chance? Or will [CBS entertainment president at that time] Jeff (Trigger Finger) Sagansky have second thoughts by next Thursday when the series goes into its regular time slot?"

Network dramas do have a high mortality rate because they need time to cultivate an audience — time a network is reluctant to spend when faced with low ratings. Shows such as *Hill Street Blues* and *Homicide* barely survived their first seasons, only to go on to enjoy long runs; but they are the exceptions. As it turned out, however, both critics and fans embraced *Second Chances*. "You've got to like a show like this spunky new serial that hits the ground sprinting," wrote David Hiltbrand in *People*, who graded it a B. "As we are introduced to the two main characters, sisters played by Connie Sellecca and Megan Porter Follows, each is threatening to kill a different man. Okay, they're probably only blowing off steam, but these are clearly not women to be trifled with. *Second Chances* isn't as saucy or subversive as *Picket Fences*, and the show's scope is a little narrow. But it is impertinent and eventful. And it has an appealing ensemble which includes Ronny Cox, Michelle Phillips, Jennifer Lopez and Justin Lazard."

Of course, not everyone was so enchanted. Ken Tucker of *Entertainment Weekly* found the show contrived and predictable. "Somewhere along the line, eternally slinky Michelle Phillips pops up just long enough to hop into bed with — no, that would be giving away one of the few plot turns you can't see coming way ahead of time. *Second Chances* relies on too many verbal clichés and pat coincidences to promise much in the way of engrossing escapism."

Airing opposite *L.A. Law*, the series was ranked in the mid-fifties. That's good by today's standards, but this was in the days before UPN and the WB existed and cable was a powerful programming force. In other words, *Second Chances* was struggling to find an audience. And because of that, it became one of the first shows to make use of the Internet. Beginning the night of its premiere, December 2, 1993, *Second Chances* became a hot chat-room topic — a fact not lost on Dorothy Swanson, president of Viewers for Quality Television, who picked up on it and slipped a last-minute plug for the show into the newsletter she was about to mail to the members of her organization. Said Swanson, the Internet "gives me a head start. The feedback is immediate."

The potential of this new communications medium was being pondered by some future-thinking CBS executives. Senior Vice President for Marketing and Communications George Schweitzer saw something urgent in the dozens of CompuServe postings where viewers eagerly discussed *Second Chances* plot developments. Here was a window on fan interest that the archaic Nielsen rating was incapable of accessing. "That's critical information for me," said Schweitzer — so critical that he would later insist to Jeff Sagansky that he take a look and see for himself what viewers were saying in their Internet postings.

But, regardless of how many people were watching, being the third lead on a primetime series was winning Jennifer Lopez more attention than she'd ever had. In December of 1993, the University of Wisconsin team traveled west to play in college football's Rose Bowl game on New Year's Day. Prior to the big game, the university marching band was invited to take part in a parade at Disneyland to honor the players from Wisconsin. Several hundred fans who had also traveled to California for the game were on hand that day. It was the first time in thirty years that the school had qualified for the Rose Bowl, so everyone was pumped. For those fans back home in icy Wisconsin, the Disneyland parade was to be broadcast on January 1, an hour before the Tournament of Roses Parade, as part of a CBS special called *Coming up Roses*. And selected to host the special were Doug Davidson from *The Young and the Restless* and Jennifer Lopez from *Second Chances*. Sitting behind a rose-bedecked podium under the warm California sun, watching the band on parade, Jennifer must have felt she'd come a very long way from the Bronx.

Thanks, in large part, to the show's vocal fans, CBS decided to grant *Second Chances* the time necessary to establish itself, but the network wanted the romance quotient of the show upped. Latham and Lechowick complied by signing ex-*Dukes of Hazzard* heartthrob John Schneider to play handsome construction executive Pete Dyson, who takes over the bankrupt business that Dianne has inherited from her late husband. With the addition of Schneider and the support of the network, the series seemed to be on track.

But what the cast and network didn't know was that Connie Sellecca was harboring a very big secret. She and husband John Tesh were expecting a baby. Her main reason for not immediately telling the show's producers was that she'd suffered a miscarriage in August 1993, and she wanted to wait until her first trimester had passed before announcing her pregnancy. However, when pressed, she also admitted that she'd been worried that the network people might have been less inclined to pick up the show for the next season if they'd known she was pregnant.

It wasn't an easy secret to keep. "I was very sick, which made working that much more difficult," Sellecca revealed in a *Good Housekeeping* interview. "I tried to run to my dressing room before I threw up." Of course, it's almost impossible to keep a secret on a film or television set; someone overheard Sellecca gagging in the bathroom and reported it to the producers. Aware that a pregnancy might impact negatively on their renewal decision, the producers guarded Connie's secret. Then, once CBS had given the green light for more episodes, Sellecca and Tesh made their announcement. And Jennifer Lopez was on the brink of becoming a genuine television star.

Then suddenly, at 4:31 A.M. on January 17, 1994, everything changed. The Northridge earthquake hit with such force that chimneys snapped off houses. Tables flew across rooms and splintered against walls. Sleepers awoke to find themselves on the floor and groped for something to hold on to until the shaking was over. When the earth finally stopped moving, it was obvious to longtime residents that this had been a bad one. Not the dreaded Big One that geologists keep predicting, but bad. The worst-hit areas were in the San Fernando Valley. Because of the type of soil there, liquefaction occurred — the earth beneath the houses literally dissolved under the stress. The floor of the valley moved many inches north and the mountains grew an astonishing fifteen inches in height. It was an awe-inspiring display of nature's power, and it affected everyone and everything in its path. Celebrity counted for nothing. Warren Beatty and Annette Bening's hilltop house, with its huge windows overlooking the San Fernando Valley, was reduced to a large pile of glass shards.

Jennifer Lopez came through unscathed, but the production facility where *Second Chances* was filmed — in Valencia, about twenty minutes north of the valley — suffered extensive damage. Even so, the show's producers and CBS expected production to go forward. The earthquake had forced CBS to juggle its schedule, however; *Second Chances* was taken off the air for six weeks and replaced by a George C. Scott vehicle called *Traps*, which had been panned by the critics.

Gail Pennington of the St. Louis *Post-Dispatch* wryly noted, "The best news about *Traps* is that after six episodes, it will vanish to be replaced by the returning *Second Chances*. That Connie Sellecca mystery-soap had lots going for it and was slowly building a cult following when its sets and production facilities were badly damaged in the Los Angeles earthquake. Rebuilding has been slow, but the network has maintained its order of twenty-two episodes, which should keep *Chances* running into the summer — time, maybe, for a bigger audience to find it."

Unfortunately, the damage proved too great to overcome. "We thought we'd come up running," said Lechowick, "but at first we couldn't even get into our production facilities, and when we did, we found that water from burst overhead pipes had ruined everything." The twenty-two-episode order was cut to nine, with the final installment airing "late one night after Letterman." Despite everyone's desire to keep the show going and to film the full twenty-two episodes, the production was officially canceled.

Although she was bitterly disappointed, Jennifer knew she couldn't struggle against an act of God. Plus, she had reason to be optimistic. The series had given her the chance to show that she was more than just a dancer. It had also made her one of the few Latin actresses to be seen on prime time, and she seemed very much at home in that setting. Certainly CBS, as well as Lynn Marie Latham and Bernard Lechowick, had recognized a special quality in Jennifer, and it wasn't long before she was back in business with them.

The network asked Latham and Lechowick to develop another series, but they needed some time to refocus. While many writer-producers have stacks of project proposals at hand, that wasn't how this particular team operated. "We only work on one project at a time — we give it our all," Lechowick commented. That wasn't to say that they had no ideas. "We're always doing research," continued Lechowick, "and we'd been collecting information about the hotel-restaurant business for a full three years, interviewing any employee who'd talk to us when we were on vacation with the kids or just out to dinner."

One thing that jumped out at them from their unofficial study was that people who worked in that industry liked their jobs. "Everyone you know is always saying, 'Gosh, I wish I were a — blank.' But here we found job satisfaction. They said, 'Every day is different; you never know what's going to happen.' And so we thought, 'Let's portray this interesting life, focusing on the folks who work in the hotel, not the guests.'" Lechowick and Latham also liked the *Upstairs, Downstairs* idea of interweaving the lives of the wealthy owners with the lives of their employees. However, they wanted to add a dimension: "By hard work and effort, Downstairs can rise to Upstairs."

The network gave the series an initial six-episode order. In the lineup of characters were two holdovers from *Second Chances* — Jennifer's Melinda Lopez character and her father, Sal, played by Pepe Serna. Jennifer's personal appeal helped open the door to this opportunity, but another important factor was that CBS agreed with the show's producers that television didn't have enough strong, Hispanic families as it was; they didn't want "to let this one [Melinda and Sal Lopez] die." The new series was called *Hotel Malibu*, and it was set in a family-run hotel. Gail Pennington of the St. Louis *Post-Dispatch* announced the new series by saying, "Their last series was canceled by Mother Nature. But second chances do happen in Hollywood, so Bernard Lechowick and Lynn Marie Latham are back with another of their hard-to-describe, easy-to-watch romantic-comedy-drama-whodunits. CBS booked a stay at *Hotel Malibu* on the strength of the creators' credentials and a one-sentence description: *Upstairs, Downstairs* in a California beach hotel."

The series starred Joanna Cassidy as Elly Mayfield, the widowed, still-grieving owner of the hotel. But Elly's pining days are numbered when she hooks up with her old high-school sweetheart, Sal Lopez. John Dye played her scheming son, and Cheryl Pollak played her daughter, who has come home to work in the family business. Consider them the *Upstairs* characters. The *Downstairs* denizens included Harry O'Reilly as a hardworking bartender, Romy Windsor as his extremely ambitious sister, and Jennifer Lopez as the bartender trainee.

As cast and crew got down to work, Jennifer got a lesson in the business of television. Simply put, the quality of the finished product is but one factor in the process of making or breaking a series. Veterans Lechowick and Latham had learned this lesson long ago. They'd learned to spend lots of time promoting their own work, since "we can't have an impact on how the network promotes us." Lechowick adds, "a television series can fall victim to many things — competition, time slot, one never knows." But no show can succeed unless people actually tune in. "I compare a series on television to a new cereal on the shelf," says Lechowick. "You've seen those cereal sections; they're seven feet tall, thirty yards long. Even if your cereal tastes good and is nutritious, you still have to get people to taste it. It's exactly the same for a television show. But we feel very strongly that if people try it, they'll like it."

Not if they're misled, however. For years CBS had been trying, and failing, to draw in younger viewers. Courting that sector of the television audience, the network ran promos for *Hotel Malibu* that gave the impression the series was going to be a raunchy beach version of *Melrose Place*. "If you tell the audience something that's not reflective of the actual content, it will do two things," explains Lechowick. "It will make those who show up unhappy. And it will keep others from showing up at all. So we're adamant about telling the public how we define our work."

What Lechowick felt they did was tell stories. "The true asset of the one-hour format and ensemble cast is that it allows all kinds of storytelling — some happy, some sad; comedy, tragedy, farce. We try to make you laugh, break your heart, intrigue you and also do serious-issue stories. On *Homefront*, our Emmy-nominated episode dealt with a Holocaust survivor's memories. Even on *Knot's*, we did a teen-drug story line that was used in schools, and also a rape story that focused on the survival of the victim. Telling stories of survival, heroic survival and the day-to-day kind, that's our style."

Jennifer could relate to that approach. She hadn't been able to pursue commercial work because she didn't believe in what she was hocking, and so she respected Lechowick and Latham for writing material that mattered and had depth. Or at least for trying to.

The underlying theme of the series was the struggle to start over. And what better place to do that than Malibu? Nancy, the bartender's sister, has left her job as a real estate agent to seek more down-to-earth work, becoming a room attendant; Stevie, Elly's daughter, has just been fired from her advertising job; and Melinda has just quit her job at another hotel, where she isn't considered "blond enough," and is hired to work behind the Hotel Malibu bar, despite her complete lack of experience. All three women start work on the same day, and it becomes obvious to them almost immediately that something is amiss: the hotel is up for sale and supposedly losing money, even though it's filled to capacity.

The first week it aired, *Hotel Malibu* ranked twenty-fourth in the ratings. But the second week it plummeted to the forty-second position, meaning that a significant number of people who watched the first week chose not to tune in again — never a good sign for a producer.

Although there were some kind reviews — Mike Hughes of Gannett News Service said that "*Malibu* crackles with fun" and called Lopez and Serna "people to care about" — *Hotel Malibu* found little favor with audiences and even less with critics.

"Who does the hiring at this swank beachfront resort? Mr. Magoo?" asked David Hiltbrand in *People*. "The staff is made up of swindlers, dumb straight arrows, snakes and seductresses. Good help can't be this hard to find, even in California." But he did reserve kind words for the cast. "Apart from the exotic employees, this summer series from the creators of *Homefront* and *Second Chances* is a middling melodrama with a winning cast — among them, Joanna Cassidy, Harry O'Reilly, and Jennifer Lopez."

Ken Tucker of *Entertainment Weekly* was brutal and brief in his analysis, saying that the show's "characterizations are thin, the plot developments banal." *Newsday*'s Marvin Kitman was more thoughtful in his assessment: "If you ask me, the basic trouble with the Lechowicks is they aren't trashy enough for TV. They can't write trashy. Their people don't have that magical combination of vapidity and stupidity that appeals to Generation X. They keep trying to go down market with their stories — from *Homefront* to *Hotel Malibu* the direction has been going south. But they are still too good for young people [and] not good enough for soap-opera snobs like myself."

So, with no intention of renewing the summer series for its regular-season schedule, CBS aired the six episodes of *Hotel Malibu* between August 4 and September 8. Despite the failure of *Second Chances* and *Hotel Malibu* to become hits, CBS was still anxious to continue its association with Lopez, and the network offered her an attractive development deal of her own. It's especially hard for a young actor to turn down such a lucrative offer, but Jennifer knew that she didn't want to take her career in this direction. She declined the offer.

During her time working in television she'd learned a lot, but now she had her sights set on a bigger goal. Jennifer Lopez was ready to make her dream of being a movie star come true.

4

One of the Family

Although it's clear that CBS executives were impressed with Jennifer's charisma and screen appeal, their efforts to sign her to a development deal also had an ulterior political motive. In September 1994 a study commissioned by a Latino advocacy group called the National Council of La Raza presented its findings. They showed that Hispanics were less visible on prime time in the mid-1990s than they had been during the 1950s, when Desi Arnaz Jr. and shows such as *Zorro* were having an impact. Despite making up almost ten percent of the American population, Hispanics comprised only one percent of all characters portrayed during the 1992–93 season. In contrast, African Americans, who account for twelve percent of the general population, were seen in seventeen percent of television roles.

"Hispanics remain virtually invisible in prime-time entertainment. The proportion of Latino characters has been declining since the 1950s," said S. Robert Lichter who coauthored the fifty-five-page report *Distorted Reality: Hispanic Characters in TV Entertainment*. More disturbing were the statistics suggesting that when Latins did appear they were usually shown in an unsavory light, playing criminals or drug addicts. Of the Hispanic characters who were seen, sixteen percent committed crimes, compared with only four percent of both blacks and whites.

"This is systematic slander," said Raul Yzaguirre, president of the National Council of La Raza. "We're very concerned about the negative portrayal of Hispanics." The greatest offenders were such shows as *Cops*, *Top Cops*, and *American Detective*. "Basically, these shows consist of whites arresting minorities," Lichter charged. For Yzaguirre, it wasn't a matter of cultural or ethnic pride, nor, he insisted, was it about "one group trying to get more attention. It's about defining America. Television is robbing an entire society of reality. We're putting the networks on notice."

Of the networks, Fox and ABC fared the worst; each was given an F. And NBC earned a D, while CBS got off with a C. The shows singled out for portraying Hispanics in a positive way included *L.A. Law, Hot Squad, Law & Order, Golden Palace, The John Larroquette Show, Hotel Malibu, Beverly Hills 90210,* and *Nurses.* In a bit of irony, all but *90210,* and *Law & Order* were canceled at the end of the season reviewed.

It was the beginning of a fight that has yet to come to a satisfying resolution, although, if nothing else, raising the issue of the balanced representation of minorities on television and in film sparked a long-overdue dialogue. Gregory Freeman of the St. Louis *Post-Dispatch* thoughtfully noted that the networks were hesitant to present series peopled by minorities, "partly because they're afraid of how the audience might react and partly because they're afraid, period — TV executives often seem unimaginative when it comes to providing programming. For blacks, the majority of programs featuring them are comedies. While comedies are fine, a balance is needed. Dramatic and other types of programming would go far in presenting well-rounded pictures of African-Americans in this country. But, for whatever reason, Hollywood has been slow to react to the increasing diversity in America. For blacks, that's often meant silly programming designed to appeal to the lowest common denominator. But for Hispanics, it has often meant no portrayals at all or portrayals as criminals."

Freeman went on to point out that the presence of blacks on television began to increase "during the peak of the civil rights movement, during the 1960s," and that in order for change to occur some noise has to be made. In conclusion, Freeman noted that "It's too bad that anyone should have to say anything at all about Hollywood's portrayals. But the entertainment industry is one that traditionally has been built on stereotypes. The only way to battle those stereotypes is to stand up and be counted."

At the same time, some well-respected Latin actors don't want to limit themselves creatively. Jimmy Smits, who has enjoyed a very successful television career thanks to *L.A. Law* and *NYPD Blue,* says, "As an artist you have that other thing going on. I can't be thinking about holding this role-model-flag and have that affect my decisions. As an actor you want to be versatile, and I can't just be playing Hispanics all the time. And as far as the role model is concerned, I'd be really limiting myself if I called my agent and said I only want to play good guys. That would be very limiting."

At this point in her career, Jennifer felt that the best way to proceed was to do good work and refuse to let her ethnic heritage stand in the way. She was proud of her Puerto Rican background, but at the same time she believed that she was just as American as the girl next door. However, it would take a strongly Hispanic role to break her out and turn casting agents color blind when they looked her way.

In taking on that role, she would be contracting to work with the man who would later cast her in the role that would make her a star. Gregory Nava first captured the attention of the Hollywood film industry with his 1983 independent film *El Norte*, arguably the first American feature to present Latins as three-dimensional characters. The film followed a Guatemalan brother and sister as they flee their troubled homeland and make their way to *El Norte* — the United States. The movie received rave reviews, and Nava's script, which he cowrote with Anna Thomas, was nominated for an Academy Award. It not only made Nava the best-known Latin director, but it also made him the only known Latin director in Hollywood.

Nava and Thomas returned to similar themes for their next major project, called *My Family (Mi Familia)*. Except this time, the story focused on three generations of Latins — in the 1920s, 1950s, and 1980s — trying to find their place in America's complex melting-pot culture. The family history is recounted by the eldest living son, Paco (Edward James Olmos), who narrates the film.

The story begins in the 1920s with a teenaged Jose Sanchez leaving his Mexican village and traveling to Los Angeles to find his only living relative. With no means of transportation and no money, Jose has to walk to L.A. Once there, he finds his relative, who is known as El California because he is a direct descendent of the original California settlers. Jose settles in and sets out to make a life for himself in his new home.

Jose finds a job as a gardener, tending the outdoor spaces at the palaces they call homes in Beverly Hills. He meets the beautiful Maria, played in her younger years by Jennifer Lopez, who works as a housekeeper for one of his customers. The hired help are always reminded of their place in this society, but even in the face of blatant racism, Jose and Maria find love and get married with high hopes for their future. For all the problems American society has presented them with, they are still living a more prosperous life than the one Jose has left behind.

When the Great Depression hits, their dreams of a better life are destroyed. With two children to care for and a third on the way, Maria and Jose try to make do, but their peaceful world is turned upside down when Maria is picked up during an immigration sweep. She is loaded into a railroad boxcar and deported to Mexico, even though she is a United States citizen. This turn of events is more than just a dramatic device; it accurately depicts an unthinkable but common practice engaged in by the Immigration Service during that period in history.

Unaware of what has happened, Jose is frantic, but he has to keep himself together for his children. Back in Mexico, Maria is stranded, penniless, and unable to contact Jose, but she is determined to keep her family together. So, after giving birth to a son, Chucho, she embarks on the dangerous journey back to Los Angeles. It takes her almost a year, but Maria finally makes it, and the family is reunited.

The film then jumps forward to the late 1950s. Now a grown and often angry man, Chucho (Esai Morales) juggles two worlds — the America he wants to be a part of and the transplanted Mexican community whose heritage means so much to his parents. His desire to indulge in pop culture infuriates his old-school father, and it is a constant source of conflict between father and son. Also, Chucho sees his father as someone who has allowed himself to become downtrodden, something Chucho will never let happen. As a result, he presents himself as the toughest hombre in the neighborhood, although for the most part it's pure posturing. As the family prepares for the wedding of the oldest daughter, Irene (Maria Canals), Chucho's defiance leads to a tragedy from which the family will never completely recover. He gets involved in a fight with his sworn enemy, Butch (Michael De Lorenzo), which leads to his own death at the hands of some overzealous police officers.

The last third of the film takes place in the 1980s, and it follows the youngest son of Maria and Jose, Jimmy (Jimmy Smits), who has been psychologically scarred by the death of his older brother Chucho. When the audience first meets Jimmy, he is being pressured into an arranged marriage. His social-activist sister Toni (Constance Marie) and brother-in-law David (Scott Bakula) want him to marry a young immigrant woman, Isabel (Elpidia Carrillo), in order to prevent her from being deported. At first Jimmy tries to avoid any kind of relationship with Isabel at all, only to find himself falling in love with her. Then tragedy strikes again: Isabel dies during childbirth. Having to deal with another terrible loss sends Jimmy into a fury, and he completely divorces himself from his newborn son, Carlitos.

Five years pass. Jimmy has been in prison. Upon his release, he returns home hoping to salvage his relationship with his son, who has been raised by Jose and Maria. Not surprisingly, Carlitos wants nothing to do with the father who abandoned him. Jimmy has matured and his anger has been replaced by compassion. He keeps reaching out to his son, and Carlitos eventually lets go of his own anger and accepts his father's love.

Jennifer, having grown up in the Bronx, was more familiar with the trials of Puerto Rican immigrants than those of Mexican ones, so playing Maria gave her a broader understanding of the immigrant experience. The depth and texture of the film were created out of Nava's own history. His family had lived in southern California since the 1880s, but he still had a lot of relatives in Mexico. "Although I was born and raised in San Diego — I'm a third generation native Californian — some of my immediate relatives, who live just a few miles from the house I was raised in, are Mexican. So I've always been raised in that border world, with that tremendous clash between the cultures."

Nava was well aware that Latin underrepresentation in the media was a hot-button media issue, but he refused to pitch his film as a political statement. "I see *My Family* as a film to entertain people, not to teach them," he told Dennis West of *Cineaste*. "I think that films need to entertain us, and I mean entertain in the broadest sense of the word, which is partially to enlighten us about who we are. So it is designed to be inspirational to people but it's also designed to give people a good night out at the movies. It makes you laugh, it makes you cry, it makes you feel dignity or pride, if you're a Chicano, to be Chicano."

Nava continues to maintain that audiences are ready for fresh perspectives on American culture. "I do think more new kinds of images and films need to be made," he says, "I really do. I hope that, as the society develops and more films like *My Family* get made, they will continue to be successful and we will be able to see more images up on the screen that are . . . not stereotypic but that are positive, that place us in the society and with our communities, put family in the center of our culture, which it is. Images that allow us to retain our culture — one which is thousands of years old, with very deep roots, and which has something very beautiful to contribute to the nation."

One of the things that Jennifer and other members of the *My Family* Latin cast could appreciate was the film's depiction of family life. Every day was an emotional roller coaster. "Family life, and Latino family life, is like that," says Nava. "I remember that my family would go from tragedy to comedy in the course of a day, from morning to afternoon." But, more than anything, the director wanted his film to be "life-affirming, because I think that ultimately Latino culture is a life-affirming culture, and, despite all the tragedy and discrimination and injustice, that people endure."

To counter the usual depiction of young Latin men, Nava also wanted to paint a compassionate portrait of Jimmy. "I think we're very quick nowadays, even people within the community, to dismiss this person and banish him almost. But I wanted to redeem him because I feel that nobody is beyond redemption. Our young men are valuable and important to us, and we cannot abandon them, and we have to know the trauma that they came from, and the wounds that they carry with them."

For Jennifer, making this movie was a career-affirming experience. She now knew, instinctively, that film was her medium. On screen she would truly make her mark as an actress, and not just a Latin actress. The reviews she received for playing a Mexican immigrant in Nava's film would lead to her being offered all types of roles. The reviews for *My Family* were glowing; even those reviewers who criticized aspects of the film took care to state their support for the project.

"*My Family, Mi Familia* is a grandly ambitious, warmhearted, wildly uneven movie about a Mexican-American family in East Los Angeles," wrote Caryn James of the *Minneapolis Star-Tribune*. "At its liveliest, the film seems crammed with cheerful Latin music, life-threatening immigration problems and a terrific, dominant performance by Jimmy Smits. With a deft touch that lightens the story, and the charismatic presence this film has needed all along, Smits almost single-handedly makes *My Family, Mi Familia* more engaging. And though Jimmy also faces tragedy, and estrangement from his young son, Smits brings emotional power to some predictable scenes. Much like the movie's narrator, Nava is not much of a narrator, but his story is energetic enough to survive its sometimes pedestrian telling."

Kirby Tepper of *Magill's Survey of Cinema* praised the film's balanced approach. "Director Nava and his co-author, Anna Thomas, have created a fine script which tells their tale with humor and strength. From Maria's fascination with telenovelas (the equivalent of American soap opera), to Chucho's attempts to teach the neighborhood boys how to mambo as they wash his car, to the numerous family deaths, marriages, and holidays, they bring a real sense of the events which make up the life of a family." Tepper continues: "Without avoiding the inherent problems of crime and poverty which affect the Latino community of Los Angeles, Nava has portrayed the people in the best way possible — as real people with real struggles. And he has done so with grace and humanity. The beautiful physical production of this film matches the beauty at the heart of its story, and the excellence of its actors matches the excellence of its technical staff. Bravo."

My Family, then, was a project that Jennifer could be proud to have been associated with. And, even before its release, her performance was generating enough buzz to carry her directly into another film — one that would launch Jennifer Lopez's incarnation as a sex symbol.

5

Aboard the
Money Train

As she went from working on the artistically serious *My Family (Mi Familia)* to costarring with Woody Harrelson and Wesley Snipes in *Money Train*, Jennifer got a firsthand look at the extremes of Hollywood moviemaking. While everyone who worked on *My Family* shared a sense of purpose based on the subject matter, *Money Train*'s sole reason for being was to make money. Things like plot and structure were incidental.

For the third time, Harrelson and Snipes were teaming up as celluloid buddies (this time for a reported salary of $5.5 million each), so Jennifer was hired to be the odd woman out of their two-man game. The first time Wesley and Woody had worked together on a film was in 1986. They'd participated in the Goldie Hawn comedy vehicle *Wildcats*, in which Hawn played a high-school phys-ed teacher who takes over as the coach of a rough inner-city high-school football team. As a perfect example of stretch-the-credulity-of-the-audience casting, Snipes and Harrelson played members of Hawn's team. Six years later, they would costar in the surprise hit *White Men Can't Jump*.

After that box-office bonanza, the two actors began looking for another outlet for their combined talents, although to hear them tell it, they were simply looking for a way to get paid for having a little frat-house-type fun together. In interviews, their banter was nonstop; they were getting a big kick out of themselves. When recalling their *Wildcats* experience, for example, Snipes claimed that Harrelson worked to get on Goldie's good side, so that's why Snipes befriended him in the first place. "I knew if I chummed up with him," Snipes joked during a *USA Today* interview with

Tom Green, "I'd do better since he became Goldie's pet. This guy went from having half a page [of dialogue] to whole scenes. He was the replaced quarterback, so basically it was as if he was one of those characters that dies early in the movie. That's what was supposed to happen. He was supposed to die. But Goldie liked him." Snipes then added, "I'd look at the call sheet and I'd see I've got two days off. . . . [Woody's] shooting a scene, him and Goldie. We thought they were hangin' out after the show."

According to Jon Peters, one of *Money Train*'s producers, the bantering relationship you see on screen came out of the pair's real-life rapport. "First of all they're great friends," said Peters. "Second of all, they have great timing with each other. Woody is very funny and very sweet but he's also dangerous. Wesley is charming and unpredictable. A lot of what was in the script changed because of what they did spontaneously. They have incredible chemistry together."

Money Train came along two years after the demise of *Cheers*, the television series that had given Harrelson his big career break. In the film, Harrelson and Snipes play foster brothers Charlie and John. John's family takes Charlie in as a small child and later adopts him. As a result, Harrelson's Charlie is always trying to stay in touch with his black "heritage," much to John's amusement. Explains Harrelson, "the two boys grow up together. But you can tell they haven't always gotten along. They fight a little bit. Charlie, for instance, is inclined to think that the big institutions of the world should share their wealth; John is a little more respectful of the system. This causes some friction between them."

Both brothers work as New York Metropolitan Transit Authority Police officers, and one of the film's four intersecting plot lines concerns the brothers' rivalry over fellow officer Grace Santiago, played by Jennifer Lopez. A second plot line involves their conflicts with their boss, Patterson, villainously played by Robert (*Baretta*) Blake. Patterson is an over-the-top bad guy who has it in for Charlie and John and who is obsessed with guarding the "money car" — the subway car that picks up the Transit Authority receipts — and keeping it on schedule.

The film's director, Joseph Ruben, admitted that the Transit Authority "was real nervous" about the concept of the film. "They didn't want a movie made about this train. But fortunately, Mayor Giuliani encouraged them to welcome us."

Another subplot centers on an arsonist known as The Torch, who keeps setting token booths — and the vendors inside them — on fire. Surprisingly, Grace, Charlie, and John catch The Torch long before the end of the film, leaving the fourth plot line to develop into the action climax. It turns out that Charlie is a compulsive gambler and gets himself dangerously indebted to a local mobster, who is ready to order his henchmen to break Charlie's legs — or worse.

Intensifying Charlie's desperation is his unrequited love for Grace, who finds herself more attracted to John. "She's a very attractive police officer who is also somewhat provocative to both brothers," comments Snipes. "Charlie gets the hots for her, but he basically doesn't have a snowball's chance in hell of getting her. She, of course, chooses me, which is the likely scenario."

Having been fired by Patterson, with his debt looming and the threat of physical violence hanging over him, Charlie is driven to rob the money train, thereby setting up the action finale of the film. John tries to stop Charlie from committing the crime. They argue on the train as it hurtles through the subway tunnel at breakneck speed. To Charlie, it's not really stealing because the money just goes to feed the monolithic Transit Authority, which is symbolized for him by his hated boss. But to John, it's more basic: they are cops, not robbers. Even so, he understands Charlie's misguided thinking. "The money train is visual," says Snipes, "it's consistent, and you know it's always loaded, so I can understand how Charlie could develop a strong attachment to that. It's an appealing fantasy."

Although most of *Money Train*, which cost $60 million to make, was shot on location in New York City, the extensive stunt sequences were shot on a $4.5-million, fifteen-car, half-mile-long operational subway constructed on the old Southern Pacific railway track near Chinatown in Los Angeles. "It was exactly like a real subway, except it didn't smell," Lopez told *Entertainment Weekly*'s Mark Harris. "It even had that yellowness that creeps halfway up the tiles that used to be white. It was so authentic, I felt like I could take the train home."

For Jennifer, who beat out over one hundred other actresses for the role, shooting a movie in New York was a wonderful homecoming. Director Ruben was effusive in his praise of her as he spoke of the qualities that had won her the job. "Grace had to be first of all believable as a street cop. You had to believe that she grew up in New York City, that she was a tough, strong New York cop. On top of that, she had to be one hell of an actor with humor and a lot of spirit. And Jennifer fit the bill. She's the real thing."

And others involved in *Money Train* also discovered that Jennifer didn't just play tough — she *was* tough. When she learned that her character would be carrying a .38mm revolver while John and Charlie were issued .9mms, she demanded equal firearm rights. "A .38 is such a girl gun," Lopez said, noting that she had once dated a policeman. "I'm not going to carry some sissy revolver." Duly chastened, the prop man rectified the inequity and Jennifer got her big gun.

While she may not have wanted to carry a "girl gun," Jennifer did give *In Style* magazine a glimpse of her feminine side. Asked by her interviewer to itemize the contents of her purse, she replied, "Lipstick, powder, mascara and Origins mint facial wash. I always take my cellular phone and pager, and workout gloves for the gym. Inevitably, there are stray dollar bills floating around the bottom, and tampons."

Lopez then went on to make it clear that she wasn't married to any particular look or fashion. "Going-out-at-night makeup depends on what I'm wearing, or my mood, or how I've done my hair. I'll do all different kinds of things, different looks. I like getting into the Audrey Hepburn look, or whatever. And I'm pretty good at it. I'm lucky that way. Some people are not good at putting on makeup, but I'm good with my own. Maybe it's from watching people put it on me for so long." Lopez wasn't making any claims to perfection, however. Like so many other women, she complained about dry skin and bad hair days. This willingness to reveal her unglamorous side has allowed her to project an image of accessibility — she's a regular girl who just happens to be an actress.

And that down-to-earth quality combined with a radiant natural beauty have clearly made Jennifer a guy magnet. It's not surprising that both Snipes and Harrelson became attracted to her off-camera. She would later reveal that both of her *Money Train* costars made passes at her. Harrelson she described as the more playful of the two. Speaking to Steve Rebello of *Movieline*, she recalled how she'd say, "Hey, Woody, how are you doing?" Then Harrelson would "stick out his tongue and flick it at me very nasty." On *Cheers* and in *Money Train*, Harrelson played dim but sweet characters. Off-camera, however, he was known as a womanizing party boy whose pet cause was the legalization of hemp, so such antics came as no surprise to Jennifer. She claimed that she found it funny, not

With Wesley Snipes and Woody Harrelson
at the *Money Train* premiere, 1995

offensive. And Harrelson, for his part, confessed good-naturedly, "She spurned *all* my advances."

Jennifer was less amused by Snipes's heavy-handed come-on. She candidly revealed that even though she made it clear she was still involved with David Cruz, Snipes "went full court press." She had no problem with him flirting — because, after all, "you always flirt with your costars, its harmless" — but she maintained that Snipes wouldn't take no for an answer. "He would invite us all out together and then at the end of the night, he'd drop me off last and try to kiss me," she told Rebello. "I'd be like, 'Wesley, please, I'm not interested in you like that.' He got really upset about it. His ego was totally bruised."

Lopez says her rejection of him caused a rift and that Snipes didn't speak to her for two months. To her, he was simply being "an asshole. Actors are used to getting their way and to treating women like objects. They're so used to hearing the word *Yes*." Typically, Jennifer didn't seem to care very much whether Snipes got upset with her for speaking about all of this publicly. In fact, she found it funny. "Its time for the truth to come out!"

It was also time for *Money Train* to face the critics. Overall, the reviews were mixed. What bothered reviewers most was the uneven handling of the film's four intersecting plot lines. The spectacular runaway-train ending was one of the film's strong points. And so was Jennifer Lopez. Carolyn Bingham of the *Los Angeles Sentinel* noted that while Woody Harrelson "is in the film, it's Wesley Snipes's movie from beginning to end. I'm reminded of *Passenger 57* by this film, and if you liked that, you'll like this. Don't expect another *White Men Can't Jump*. *Money Train* is a comedy/thriller, which takes buddy movies to new heights. . . . And newcomer Jennifer Lopez as Grace Santiago, a transit cop, is stunning and gives a brilliant performance. She'll open many doors for Hispanic female actresses."

Others thought Jennifer's talents had been squandered. *Minneapolis Star Tribune* film critic Jeff Strickler wrote, "The problem is the set-up. Even if you haven't seen the TV commercials, it's obvious where the plot is headed. But director Joseph Ruben (*Sleeping with the Enemy*), working from a script by Doug Richardson (*Die Hard 2*) and David Loughery (*Passenger 57*), allows the story to dawdle. Ruben appears to have three goals for the prolonged set-up. He overdoes one, gives the second short shrift and plays the third by the numbers. . . . And he needs to work in a little romance (namely, sex). The opportunities provided by Jennifer Lopez are not developed; her character seems like an afterthought. You may be tempted to doze off during the film's lengthy preliminary stretches. Go ahead; you won't miss much. Just make sure someone wakes you for the payoff."

Newsday's John Anderson proclaimed *Money Train* to be a guilty-pleasure kind of film. "The [Manhattan Transit Authority] stuff alone is enough to make me dismiss all the illogic, bad taste and questionable criminal activity. Cops as thieves, instruction on how to torch token vendors, one overheated sex scene and a sprinkling of gratuitous violence: *Money Train* has everything a holiday movie needs. Even the subway system isn't portrayed quite rightly — which is probably wise, given how many knuckleheads might want to hijack a real money train. But this is a popcorn movie that basically does what it's supposed to, even if you have to overlook a lot — like the climactic train chase itself: If Patterson wanted to stop the train, wouldn't he just cut the power? Oh, well. Details, details. The subway system should run as well as this movie."

Then, four days after the movie's November 22, 1995 opening, a horrendous criminal act destroyed the sense of fun and fantasy that *Money Train* had been designed to project. In the film, Chris Cooper played the arsonist who set token booths on fire by squirting a flammable liquid into them and then igniting it. On November 26, a clerk at a Brooklyn subway station fell victim to a copycat attack, suffering life-threatening burns. Three days later, a similar attack was made at another station, but no one was hurt.

The fact was, there had been assaults like these on token booths prior to the release of *Money Train*, and the authorities had already outfitted booths with flame-smothering equipment. If anything, the writers of *Money Train* had borrowed from real life. However, whenever a crime can be linked to a film or a television show, certain politicos will see it as a good opportunity for a sound bite and some strategic posturing. Following what were being called "the *Money Train* attacks," Senator Bob Dole urged Americans to boycott the film during a speech he made from the Senate floor. Dole would be a contender in the 1996 presidential race, and he made the slackening of Hollywood morality a favorite campaign theme.

Such obviously opportunistic rabble-rousing angered many involved with the film's production, including Lopez, who wasn't afraid to speak out.

"It's a terrible crime, and our hearts go out to the victim," *People* quoted her as saying. She then added that Dole's offensive confused her. "People see so many violent movies. Why would they pick that scene from *Money Train*? In a way, you think the film is responsible, but it's not. It's the criminals." In conclusion she reflected, "It just made me more conscious of what I would do in other movies. You have such an influence over people, it's kinda scary."

In a very short while, Jennifer would witness an even more vivid demonstration of just how much a film can influence the audiences that flock to see it. In May 1995, a young Tejano singer named Selena was shot and killed by the president of her fan club. Although the tragedy made little impact on most white Americans, in the Latin community Selena's murder was a horror on a par with that of John Lennon's. Even if few Hollywood executives knew who Selena was before her death, they were smart enough to recognize the dramatic potential of her life story, especially since the high-profile media coverage had made Selena far more famous dead than she had been alive. So, in August of 1995, Selena's father, Abraham Quintanilla, issued a press release announcing that he would be acting as executive producer in a joint venture involving his Q Productions, Moctesuma Esparza, and Robert Katz, who had produced *Gettysburg*. The project was a film based on Selena's life. Gregory Nava, the cowriter and director of *My Family (Mi Familia)*, would write and direct the biopic, which was scheduled to begin filming the following February. An international casting call was planned to find the right actress to play Selena.

At the time of this announcement, Jennifer Lopez already had a full cinematic plate. She had just completed filming *Jack*, directed by Francis Ford Coppola, and was on location in Miami shooting *Blood and Wine* with Jack Nicholson and Michael Caine.

Lopez was aware that she had dodged a career bullet with *Money Train*. "I was the only one who came out of that movie smelling like a rose," she acknowledged. Asked why she was suddenly being hired by A-list directors, she offered this explanation: "People just seem to respond to me when I go in to read for them. The same weekend Francis Ford Coppola hired me for *Jack* and I got *Blood and Wine* after auditioning for Bob Rafelson six times. It just happens, I don't know why. There must be something you consciously do that impresses these legendary directors. It's all about controlling the emotion, you know? Anybody can scream, anybody can cry. It's about just being in the moment and doing whatever comes natural."

But as the roles she auditioned for, and won, steadily improved, her personal life was suffering. David Cruz, her high-school sweetheart and the first love of her life, was to become the first romantic victim of Jennifer's career — although he would not be the last. Stephanie Cozart Burton, a makeup artist for *In Living Color*, remembers Cruz as "sweet but not quite ready for prime time, like the high school boyfriend who was going to get left behind."

To Lopez, they were just a typical, if painful, example of two people growing in different ways. As Jennifer's star ascended, Cruz, who had found work as a production assistant, seemed directionless. Jennifer could not abide the inequity. "He came out here with me and was here with me the whole time when I first started doing television," she told *People* magazine's Kyle Smith. "Career-wise, we weren't in the same place. He just didn't know what he wanted to do. But I had a fire under my ass. I was so fast, I was like a rocket; he was like a rock."

Although powerfully determined not to let anything, or anyone, prevent her from pursuing her dreams and realizing her ambitions, Jennifer would discover that, for all her success, finding a partner who would complement her life and her career would be a heartbreaking task.

6

The Big Time

While Francis Ford Coppola will forever be revered in Hollywood as the creative force behind the *Godfather* trilogy, his work over the past two decades has been spotty, both commercially and artistically. It was somewhat surprising that he would venture into comedy with the film *Jack* — Coppola had been called many things in the course of his career but "laughmeister" wasn't one of them. Still, the five-time Academy Award winner is a director few performers pass up an opportunity to work with. When he chose Jennifer over Ashley Judd to play Robin Williams's schoolteacher in *Jack*, she was understandably honored and excited.

Jack can't really be described as a pure comedy, because its central story concerns a child who will die an untimely death. Coppola said he didn't regard Jack's disease as "literally a genetic disease." Instead, the director was aiming to create an allegory about learning tolerance and about the perils of growing up too fast. "All of us are kind of like Jack," Coppola noted. "Our lives are whizzing by."

The movie begins at a costume party, where Jack's dad is dancing with his pregnant wife in a conga line. Both are shocked when her water breaks, because she's only a few months pregnant. It becomes clear early on that something is very wrong with Jack; his cells are growing at four times the normal rate, resulting in an accelerated maturation process. However, while his body ages rapidly, his mental maturation is that of a normal child. By the time Jack is ten, he's turned into Robin Williams.

Worried that Jack will be ridiculed at school, his parents — played by Brian Kerwin and Diane Lane — have Jack tutored at home by a kind teacher named Mr. Woodruff, played by Bill Cosby. Despite Cosby's super-star status on television, his film career had been less than remarkable. It took some convincing to get Cosby to participate in the project. "My agent felt the part was excellent for me," he says, "because the fellow's person-ality was similar to my own. And I met with Francis but I thought both he and my agent were wrong. I accepted the part — to prove them wrong!" What it came down to, however, was that Cosby had built a career for himself out of being in touch with his inner child, and *Jack*'s fable-like qual-ity appealed to him.

Mr. Woodruff gently suggests to Jack's parents that they send their son to public school. "Jack makes life fresh and different for my character," Cosby notes. "As his tutor, I suggest that Jack should go out into the real world and take the blows. Woodruff really wants to protect Jack. But he catches himself and has to think about what is best for his pupil. Woodruff's toughest decision is to say, 'This kid should enjoy life — have the stones thrown at him, as well as the roses.' And if Woodruff doesn't let the boy go out into the real world, the tutor could very well be responsible for this person living fast in chronological human being years, and dying, knowing nothing more about life than the family car and house. So it's a very impor-tant decision for the character to make."

Despite her misgivings, Jack's mom takes him to the local school, where he's introduced to the principal and his new teacher, Miss Marquez, played by Lopez. She helps Jack and his classmates get used to each other. Naturally, Jack is regarded as an oddity at first, but soon enough his class-mates clue in to the advantages of having a kid around who can pass as an adult. Once they give Jack half a chance, they can begin to appreciate him as a person.

For some reason, the full implications of his condition have never occurred to Jack, but he eventually realizes that if he looks forty when he's ten, in another decade he'll possess an eighty-year-old body. This glimpse of his mortality compels him to ask Miss Marquez to go to the school dance with him. When she gently turns him down, Jack is so devastated that the stress gives him an angina attack and he's hospitalized. But, with the support of his parents, his school friends, and his teachers, Jack chooses to seize the day and live whatever time he has left to the fullest. The movie ends with a grandfatherly looking seventeen-year-old Jack giving a life-affirming commencement address as class valedictorian.

Jack was a change of pace for Jennifer. It was also the first project in which she had been given a part not specifically written for a Latin actress. Coppola had seen her work in *My Family (Mi Familia)* and had sought her out for the crucial role of Jack's first school teacher and the object of his first (and perhaps only) romantic crush. "Jack is allowed to go to school for the first time and comes to my classroom," says Lopez. "At first, the kids are cruel to him, and afraid of him, because he's big; the size of a forty-year-old man. And Jack feels quite alone, because he really is just a boy. My character is kind of his saving grace. She's there for him when he's lonely and makes sure the other kids don't pick on him. What's most fascinating to my character, Miss Marquez, is how normal Jack looks. But when you look into his eyes, you can tell he's a boy."

Lopez had only praise for costar Robin Williams, calling him "an incredible actor, as well as a brilliant comedian. He's made it so easy to believe that there is a little boy hiding inside that big body. You get completely taken in."

Jennifer also remarked that had Jack really been a grown man, her character could have easily ended up in a relationship with him. "Physically, they could probably be a great couple together, but mentally, he's a boy and she's a grown woman." So, instead of a romance, they have a communion of souls. "There are great things that happen between the two of them; tragic things, too. That's what makes the story so beautiful. It's the comedy, tragedy and the sweetness of life. The tragedy of Jack's life is that he probably will never have a romantic relationship. Miss Marquez realizes that, and it breaks her heart. It's a heart-breaking story. Jack is cheated out of a lot of things that we all get to experience in life — the joys of life."

Even though the movie is fanciful, Cosby believes the emotional undertones have been grounded in real life to the extent that "people can identify with it completely. This is the kind of movie, like *Alice in Wonderland* and *Gulliver's Travels*, where they can remember how to find the hidden meaning in things, to find love and warmth, to feel good about themselves. And there's a lot of fun and games in the movie, once Jack breaks out and starts to get with the other kids. It's a wonderful picture."

Before he started to shoot the film, Coppola asked the actors — including the fifteen young performers who were to play Jack's fifth-grade schoolmates — to come to his Napa Valley, California, home for two weeks of rehearsals. Not only did this give them all time to immerse themselves in their characters — the director insisted that everyone stay in character for the duration of their stay — but it also gave the actors time to get comfortable being around one another.

"It was an incredible experience," Jennifer recalls, adding, "I'm a city girl, and there must have been too much clean air, or something, because I got a little ill." But she was too intrigued by the acting exercise to let a little bug keep her down. "We were in that world — Jack's world, which lent itself to the kind of special things — the magic — that happened. We had such a great time. We got to know each other as our characters. It was a process I hadn't been through with any other director. I taught class to the boys," she says. "They'd get out of hand, the way that boys do, but it went well. And they taught me a thing or two."

One of the hardest aspects of being an actor is to witness a project that begins with such promise fail to achieve what you imagined it would. For as wonderful as the rehearsal and filming processes were, *Jack* did not ignite the audience or the critics. But, just as she had with *Money Train*, Jennifer came away from the exercise enriched by the experience and untainted by association.

Jack has "two redeeming features," wrote critic John Simon. "The enchanting Diane Lane as Jack's mother, and the no less enchanting Jennifer Lopez as a sympathetic teacher. But though these lovely ladies and fine actresses salvage much, it is nowhere near enough." Matt Roush of *USA Today* commented, "When it comes to the cold-blooded Corleones, *Godfather* director Francis Ford Coppola knows from family values. But the formerly formidable film titan flops as a mush-meister with this *Big*-style fable about a ten-year-old who grows four times faster than normal. The film grows old even quicker than that. Bad movies happen. But when bad movies happen to good people, it's worse."

Newsday critic Jack Matthews took offense at the very premise of the film. "First-time writers James DeMonaco and Gary Nadeau are pushing messages about the fleetingness of youth and the quality of life. It's not how many years we get, but what we do with them. . . . Fable or not, it was a terrible idea to fictionalize a real disease whose victims we've seen as balding, birdlike children with transparent skin and use it as a device for a situation comedy. The clinical backdrop makes it hard not to compare those sad images with that of the robustly healthy Williams, or to forget that we're being asked to fall in love with a doomed child. . . . Little need be said about Coppola's direction. The film is so ordinary in its staging and execution it could have been done by any journeyman director in Hollywood. *Jack* may be about making the most of what you've got, but it's distinguished by how much talent it squanders."

Some fans and critics, though, did appreciate the message the movie was trying to send. "Very few actors would be up to the challenge of portraying Jack," said reviewer James M. Welsh. "But Robin Williams has specialized in odd and offbeat demanding roles, and he is perfect here. This movie has a heart as big as the Ritz and is entertaining as well as thoughtful." Welsh went on to proclaim *Jack* as "one of the summer's very best family films, equally amusing for children and adults."

For once, a movie Jennifer had appeared in hadn't generated political controversy. Off-camera, however, she had taken political action. As part of the twenty-five-member executive committee of Artists for a Democratic Victory Committee, she found herself working shoulder-to-shoulder with the likes of Maya Angelou, Barbra Streisand, William and Rose Styron, Lauren Bacall, and Rosie O'Donnell. Along with her fellow committee members, she signed a letter intended to recruit more celebrities to the cause, get the voters out, and generally whip up some political enthusiasm. "The stakes are high this year," the letter read. "Freedom of expression, freedom of choice and the rights of privacy we cherish as Americans and artists are threatened."

If ever an actress set about making her mark at just the right political moment, it was Jennifer Lopez. Not only were the film and television industries opening up their doors but also the publishing world was beginning to take notice of the country's largely untapped Latin consumer market. Over the next few years several big-name publishers would develop divisions devoted exclusively to that market; magazines geared towards Latin issues — from social to personal — began to appear on the newsstands. Christy Haubegger, president and publisher of *Latina*, remembers what it was like growing up seeing nothing but blue-eyed blond models in magazines. "I always was a voracious magazine reader, yet I had never seen makeup articles that featured brown eyes or almond skin," she told Anita McDivitt of the *Dallas Morning News*.

Haubegger, a twenty-seven-year-old Mexican American from Houston, Texas, pitched the idea of a Latin women's magazine to over one hundred and fifty prospective investors, but she'd only raised $250,000 of the $5 million she needed to launch the magazine. Then Haubegger sent her proposal to Edward Lewis, who years before had started *Essence* magazine, the high-profile and very successful magazine for African-American women. "It was one of the best, most professional business proposals I've seen in twenty-five years," Lewis told Elizabeth Llorente of *Her Latina Self*. "Haubegger is an outstanding saleswoman. She's hard-working, ethical, dedicated. She had to do this. It reminded me of myself when I was in my twenties, talking about starting *Essence*."

According to Lewis, Haubegger was shocked "that no one had done for Hispanic women what they did for black women, that there was no comparable magazine for us." It didn't take a roomful of accountants to verify the economic potential of such a publication. There are more than eight million Hispanic women living in America — and their numbers will only increase over the coming years.

"The niche we're trying to fill basically didn't exist," said editor Patricia Duarte to the *Dallas Morning News*. "We're not really competing with anything else that's out there. We give them something that the other publications don't" — such as low-fat recipes for traditional Mexican dishes, articles about buying the appropriate makeup for dark skin tones, and advice on how to balance being a modern American woman with being a woman who appreciates and passes on the traditional Latin values of her parents and grandparents.

When *Latina* made its debut Jennifer Lopez wasn't yet a household name, even within the Hispanic community, but Haubegger still wanted her to be the premiere issue's cover girl. She felt that Jennifer was a good role model. "It's important that we change the images that others have of Hispanic women," said Haubegger, "but also that we present images of ourselves that are positive."

However, Haubegger made it clear that she had no intention of reserving the *Latina* cover-girl spot for celebrities like Jennifer Lopez or Gloria Estefan. For one thing, she said to Llorente, it would be impossible because famous Latin women were in short supply: "We'd have enough for just six magazines. Latinas are grossly underrepresented in all fields, despite the talent that's out there." But seeing Jennifer, a young Latin woman on the rise in a predominantly white industry, on the cover of her magazine made Haubegger proud. On a magazine stand she saw "a beautiful

Hispanic woman on the cover [of *Latina*], Jennifer Lopez right next to a cover with Claudia Schiffer. We'd done it. It sank in that we'd finally really, really done it."

Jennifer herself was too busy to spend much time pondering the political and social implications of her red-hot career. Especially since her next film, *Blood and Wine*, would team her with two of modern cinema's most important and influential artists — who also happened to belong to the clique of Hollywood's most notorious bad boys. Director Bob Rafelson and three-time Oscar-winner Jack Nicholson met at a Los Angeles film society in the mid-sixties. Despite their infamy, each is firmly established in film history. Even the fact that they cowrote the Monkees' movie *Head* only adds to their counterculture credibility. From *Easy Rider* to *Five Easy Pieces* to *The Postman always Rings Twice*, these two old friends have consistently found ways to break convention, making uncompromising films that haven't always worked but that have always been interesting.

Any actor working with Rafelson understands that they will be directed by someone who is not afraid to take risks. Which is why an actor like Nicholson tries hard to make himself available for his old friend's projects. "Jack suffers like all other movie stars, in that people want him to repeat what it is that the audience adores about him, a kind of rapscallion nature," says Rafelson. "I suppose one of the reasons why we tend to collaborate is because I say, 'Let's try something better; let's try something different; let's not have you play the same kind of guy.'"

Rafelson also told the *Independent*'s Nick Hasted, "Don't confuse entirely the part and the actor playing the part. You see Jack Nicholson in a role and thirty years later you see him in a role, and by now this routine of his has become so familiar that you wonder whether he can act or not."

The director seems to delight in his reputation as a renegade. "I can assure you, there's nothing that I have done, there's no day in my life I can remember that has been spent entirely legally," he confided to Howard Feinstein of *Newsday*. "I don't know about your life, man, but I'm gonna break the law sooner or later today! Jaywalking. My septic tank is running over right now and I'm going to hose it out. I'm not going to do it underground. And I might smoke a J or something."

While working on the 1980 Robert Redford film *Brubaker*, Rafelson was dismissed for allegedly beating up Twentieth Century Fox's head of production. "So much mythic energy has gone into me being this monster,"

Rafelson muses. "I *did* grab him, and I *did* let him go. But I did *not* hit him with thirty-seven chairs; I did not break his head open with a steel ashtray or any of the other things they had claimed I'd done." Unfazed by the implications of taking on a major studio, Rafelson sued Fox for breach of contract and slander and won. "I'd like to have my impact in movies, but I don't want it to be solely based on being a crazed psychopath."

So Jennifer had a pair of unpredictable and volatile personalities to contend with as she went into *Blood and Wine* — Rafelson and Nicholson. She also had some formidable costars — Michael Caine, Judy Davis, and up-and-comer Stephen Dorff. She couldn't afford to let herself be intimidated. "It was incredible working with Jack," she said. "I mean he's like a legend! The first time I met him it was like: 'Oh my God! That's Jack Nicholson.' I remember the first day of rehearsal. He came in, sat down and the director wanted me to sit next to him because ours was the prominent man-woman relationship in the film. Michael Caine was sitting on the other side, and I looked at one and then the other. Then it was like I had an out-of-body experience! I wondered to myself: 'What am I doing in this room with these people?' It was very scary. But fun."

Later, Lopez would tell *Good Morning America*'s Kevin Newman that when Nicholson first walked into the room she was "really, really, like, 'Oh, my God,' . . . he's such a presence. That was my third movie. And it was a big deal for me, you know. But it's something where you say to yourself, 'OK, I'm here for a reason. I'm here because they think I can do this. So if they think I can do it, I think I can do it.'"

Blood and Wine was touted as Rafelson's last installment in a loose film trilogy dealing with family problems, particularly those within father-and-son relationships. The first two parts of the trilogy were the classic *Five Easy Pieces*, released in 1970, and *The King of Marvin Gardens*, released two years later. In *Blood and Wine*, Nicholson is Alex Gates, a morally depleted wine dealer bowing under the strain of looming financial disaster. His marriage to ex-junkie Suzanne, played by Judy Davis, is crumbling fast, and his relationship with stepson Jason (Stephen Dorff) has already disintegrated — the brooding youth has nothing but disdain for his father. Alex is also embroiled in a torrid affair with a high-maintenance, luxury-loving Cuban woman named Gabriela, played by Jennifer Lopez. Rafelson claims that it wasn't until Jennifer's third audition that he "noticed she had a good body." He called her back three more times before deciding to cast her.

Initially, the script called for Jennifer to engage in a steamy love scene with Nicholson. Then it was decided that less would be more. Rafelson, in fact, was more interested in eroticism than blatant sexuality. "I try to make erotic connections between Jennifer and Stephen, and Jennifer and Jack, and even — very subtly, I hope — between Judy and Stephen, even between Judy and Jack. That puts erotic tension into every frame of the film, as opposed to, 'Let's have them get in bed.'"

According to Jennifer, "Jack thought it would be sexier if we did a little salsa dancing. He had never danced salsa before, so I had to teach him. And you know what? He never once stepped on my toes. He's a good dancer."

Certainly Nicholson's character was dancing as fast as he could. Faced with personal and professional ruin, Alex decides to steal a diamond necklace worth over one million dollars, with the help of his wheezing, emphysemic partner, Victor, portrayed by Michael Caine. Alex fantasizes about using his take from the robbery to leave his misery behind and run away with Gabriela, except she has other plans which don't include a future with Alex. Toss in the Oedipal undercurrent running between Suzanne and Jason and you have the dysfunctional dynamic in which a Rafelson film wallows. Of course, the heist goes bad and Alex's precarious existence begins an unstoppable downward plummet. "It is about someone who descends into evil," the director admitted to Hasted.

Despite the dark aspects of the story, Jennifer found Miami a wonderfully exciting place to film a movie. She enjoyed the large and lively Cuban and Latin communities of South Florida and quite unexpectedly found love in the most unlikely setting. While dining at Larios on the Beach, the superhip Miami Beach Cuban restaurant owned by Gloria Estefan, her husband, and the Larios family, Jennifer was smitten by one of the waiters. She turned to her assistant, Arlene, who had also been her best friend since grade school, and said, "That's the man I'm going to marry." Arlene says she took one look at Ojani Noa and knew Lopez meant it. However it would take a while before Jennifer would actually be introduced to Noa, who was a recent émigré from Cuba.

Now that she had her sights set on the handsome waiter, Jennifer wasn't interested in dating anyone else — a fact that upset her costar Stephen Dorff, who developed a serious crush on Jennifer. Lopez admits she flirted with Dorff a little but didn't really encourage him. So she was disappointed when he began sulking and stopped talking to her out of the pique of bruised ego. She finally told him not to "pull a Wesley on me!" after which he gave up.

While Lopez might not have been interested in her costar, she couldn't stay away from the true object of her desire. She became a regular at Larios, but was still too shy to approach Noa, in part she explains, because, "My Spanish wasn't so good, and Ojani's first language is Spanish."

Lopez admitted to *Cosmopolitan*'s Dennis Hensley that to catch Noa's eye, she did "everything in the book. I would go see him at the restaurant where he waited tables all the time and walk past him to the bathroom a million times. One time, he was coming my way, and I slipped. I was so mortified! He was like, 'Careful.'"

Finally, Jennifer's girlfriend took matters into her own hands and arranged for them to be seated at one of Noa's tables. "That night," Lopez recalls wistfully, "we went out, and it was mad love from that point on." Jennifer was sure that their passionate romance would last forever. Life was so good it was scary. Her career and her love life were blooming simultaneously. The combination gave her more confidence than ever, and this allowed her to see things in a new way.

For example, despite feeling awed at the prospect of working with Nicholson, she would take on a curiously harsh tone later, calling Nicholson "a legend in his own time and in his own mind — like the rest of us are peons." But perhaps it was the sting of the first negative reviews she had received in her brief movie career that colored her feelings.

Robert Denerstein of the *Rocky Mountain News* observed, "Rafelson infuses *Blood and Wine* with a purposefully exhausted quality, as if these characters are ready to drop in their tracks. The climate is desperate and more than a little depraved, which means the movie works but isn't a great deal of fun, except for watching Nicholson and Caine trying to out-sleaze each other. Now that's an Olympic-sized event." Then Denerstein added, "the junior members of the sleazoid firm [Dorff and Lopez] aren't quite up to speed. Early on, Lopez allows a Charo-like accent to turn her character into a bit of a caricature, but the performance settles down as the movie progresses."

Newsday's John Anderson said Lopez as Gabriela "simmers volcanic, while providing the catalyst for the Alex-Jason meltdown and proving that movie bad girls, sometimes, are simply bad. But she's not, however, the most fascinating thing about *Blood & Wine*. That prize goes to the venomous relationship between Alex and his larcenous confederate Victor Spansky (Michael Caine), a safecracker with advanced emphysema and a lethally short fuse. Rafelson makes the mistake at several points of cutting back and forth between Jason and Gabriela, waxing dreamy, and Alex and Victor, malevolently scheming and avoiding each other's horns. In terms of sheer acting, it's simply no contest."

Others felt the movie lacked the focus of Rafelson's classic films. "The script, by Nick Villiers and Alison Cross, feels fuzzy and shallow, an attempt at literary grit that fails to connect the necessary narrative dots," said Chris Vognar of the *Dallas Morning News*. "Mr. Dorff is also short-changed as a standard angry young man, drawn to the cipher-like Ms. Lopez for no apparent reason. (If he knew his stepdad was sleeping with her, we could at least chalk it up to vengeful spite.) Then there's Mr. Nicholson, an actor who faces the challenge of not playing himself every time out. He manages to turn Alex into a fairly organic character, and it's hard to blame the actor for getting stuck in a promising but ultimately limp project. It's even somewhat admirable to let Mr. Rafelson make a withdrawal from the favor bank one more time — but this is one case where it would have been better to rest on past laurels."

While it's a cliché to say that more is learned from failure than from success, it also happens to be true. Such critical questioning of her ability caused Jennifer to burn inside rather than hang her head; she couldn't wait to go out and make those critics eat their words. She already had her next film lined up. This time her vehicle would be an action-adventure flick called *Anaconda*. But it would be a role she auditioned for before *Anaconda* became a reality that would take the critics by surprise and change Jennifer's life forever.

JENNIFER LOPEZ

Entering Selena Territory

Prior to 1995, few Americans outside the Latin community knew much about Selena Quintanilla Perez. But after her murder in the spring of that year media images of her grieving fans drew attention to a phenomenon who had lived and thrived almost invisibly. Perhaps more than any other single event, Selena's death, as covered in the media, focused the nation on the Hispanic-American community and reflected a subculture that few white Americans understood. That someone like Selena could have been so successful, so beloved, and so talented and yet virtually unknown in the mainstream culture was almost as shocking as her untimely death. Tragically, Selena died before she could "cross over"; ironically Jennifer's portrayal of the singer in *Selena*, the film, would propel *her* across the cultural divide and make her the most successful female Latin star in Hollywood.

Selena Quintanilla was born in Lake Jackson, Texas, a blue-collar town not far from Houston. She lived with her two older siblings and her parents, Abraham Jr. and Marcela. Although her father had a good job — a shipping clerk at Dow Chemical — he was at heart a frustrated musician. In his younger days he had sung with a popular South Texas band called Los Dinos, and he'd never lost his passion for music and performing. So when Selena started singing, when she was about six years old, he began to fantasize about making her a star. "Her timing, her pitch were perfect," he told *People* magazine in 1995. "I could see it from day one." Selena, however, showed little interest in Latin music of any kind. She preferred Motown, pop, and country.

It's been variously reported that Abraham Quintanilla either quit his job at Dow or was laid off. Whatever the case, he left the company and opened a restaurant. As entertainment for the patrons, he had his three children — Selena, her brother, Abraham III, and her sister, Suzette — perform. After only a year the restaurant went bankrupt. It was 1981, and Abraham's enterprise, like many other small Texas businesses, was undercut by a sudden downturn in the oil industry. Not only did Abraham lose his restaurant, he lost the family home as well. "That's when we began our musical career," Selena would later recall. "We had no alternative."

The Quintanilla family moved to Corpus Christi and there they became involved in the music business. "We went to Corpus Christi to put food on the table when I was six and a half," Selena told a *Time* magazine interviewer. "We would play for family weddings. When I was eight I recorded my first song in Spanish, a country song. When I was nine we started a Tex-Mex band."

And at only nine years old, Selena went on the road with her family band, which Abraham named Selena y Los Dinos — Selena and the Guys. The guys were Selena's brother and sister and guitarist Chris Perez. Together they performed music in the style called Tejano — a bright, up-tempo, Spanish-language blend of Tex-Mex rhythms, pop-style tunes, and German polka that is hugely popular in Mexico and the Southwest. Tejano is alternatively called Tex-Mex or conjunto. The history of the genre goes back to the turn of the twentieth century, when Mexican-Americans put on country dances. Couples twirled and spun to a polka-like beat played out on accordions and big bajo-sexto guitars, which are still the main Tejano instruments.

Like any local band just scraping by, Selena y Los Dinos played anywhere, anytime — from roadhouses to weddings. "If we got ten people in one place, that was great," Selena told *People*. "We ate a lot of hamburgers and shared everything."

Although to some kids traveling around in a family band might sound like a fanciful adventure, the reality of it was something else. Selena never got to experience high school, having dropped out in the eighth grade. School dances, going out for pizza after football games, and proms were things she would only hear about. "I lost a lot of my teenage period," she acknowledged. Then she added: "But I got a lot out of it too. I was more mature." It was typical of Selena that she would dwell on the positive rather than obsess about the negative.

Over the next six years, the band managed to build a following. They started getting more profitable gigs. They also found a label willing to represent them, and they released over ten albums during that time. But everything would change abruptly in 1987, after Selena, still only fifteen, won Tejano Music Awards for Female Vocalist and Performer of the Year. Suddenly she was emerging as Tejano's brightest new star. Two years later, EMI Latin president Josa Behar signed Selena y Los Dinos to a record deal.

As she grew up, Selena developed a personal style that would become her trademark: red lipstick, long, brightly colored fingernails, tight pants, bustiers, and various stomach-revealing outfits. Due to her fashion sense and her high-energy performing style, she earned the nickname "the Tex-Mex Madonna." Her father, a Jehovah's Witness, was becoming unhappy with Selena's professional persona, but he could do little about it. To Selena, it was all part of the act and therefore okay. "What I do on stage, you won't catch me doing off stage," she explained to *Entertainment Weekly*. "Deep down, I'm still kind of timid and modest. On stage, I let go." Besides, she added, "I love shiny things and I love clothing."

And that wasn't Selena's only contradiction. The biggest irony was that this new princess of Latin pop could barely speak a word of Spanish. Her brother, A.J., would write songs for her in Spanish, and she would learn the lyrics phonetically. It wasn't until shortly after she signed with EMI that she started taking Spanish lessons, but she never developed a fluency with the language. She did, however, maintain her Texas drawl.

It seemed that anyone who saw Selena perform was smitten with her. Her legion of fans swelled. After seeing one of her concerts in San Antonio, Texas — considered the Tejano Mecca — a registered nurse named Yolanda Saldivar was so taken with the singer that she was inspired to start an official fan club. She approached Abraham Quintanilla with the idea. He had repeatedly turned down other similar offers, not being the kind of man to relinquish control over such matters easily. But Yolanda was an older fan, and she had a steady job. And although she had no children of her own and had never married (apparently never dated, either), she had taken custody of her brother's children after he abandoned them. Plus, and perhaps most importantly, she was the aunt of a childhood friend of Selena's. That, plus her unbridled enthusiasm for Selena, won Abraham over, and he granted her the (unpaid) honor of establishing Selena's official fan club.

A fan club was no small thing to Selena, who had once remarked, "Fan clubs can ruin you if people get upset and turned off by them." She was very pleased with the way hers was going and felt that Yolanda was "doing exceptionally well." When the membership grew to nine thousand in four years, Selena was impressed enough to put Saldivar in charge of the club's finances. Soon afterwards, Selena began to consider Yolanda one of her closest friends. It was a show of trust that would eventually prove fatal.

By the time she was twenty-one, Selena was a millionaire and the most popular star in Tejano music. The girl who once sang for "ten people in one place" was now performing for crowds as large as sixty thousand — as she would regularly do in Houston in the early 1990s. Thanks to Selena, annual sales of Tejano music soared between 1990 and 1995: from below seven million dollars annually to over thirty-five million. Current estimates are that the Mexican market for Tejano is worth approximately twenty million dollars a year, not only domestically but also internationally. Which is why so many major labels, including Sony, EMI, Fonovisa, Rodven, WEA Latina, and Arista have all set up Tejano divisions since Selena broke onto the scene.

Seemingly overnight, Selena had gone from living hand-to-mouth to being the Quintanilla family breadwinner. Her personal life was flourishing as well. Selena had fallen in love with her band's guitar player, Chris Perez, and the two were quietly married in 1992. Abraham Quintanilla was concerned that his daughter's marriage would discourage her young male fans and taint her youthful image. It did neither. In fact, her popularity just continued to grow, because as much as people loved her music, they seemed to love Selena, the person, even more. Her parents may have been of the conservative, traditional variety, but Selena herself was as outgoing and friendly as the average Texan. Her down-to-earth qualities were evidenced by the fact that she chose to continue living in her Corpus Christie neighborhood over moving to Houston or San Antonio. Still, she was a vibrant young woman with some extravagant tastes, so she splurged and bought herself a bright-red Porsche.

In 1994, Selena got a major career boost. *Selena Live* won a Grammy Award for best Mexican-American album. By the spring of 1995, her next album, *Amor Prohibido* (*Forbidden Love*), had sold over a half million copies domestically. Altogether, her five EMI releases had sold an estimated three million copies worldwide. "Never in my dreams would I have thought that I would become this big," she said at the time. "I am still freaking out."

But white American audiences wanted to hear songs sung in English. Musical style didn't appear to be the issue — language was the one thing that could prevent Selena (and other Latin artists, such as Ricky Martin) from achieving major success. Gloria Estefan had made American radio airwaves a safe haven for Cuban sounds; EMI believed that Selena could do the same thing for Tejano, but her next project would have to be recorded in English. Meanwhile, Selena was stretching her wings and dabbling in other areas, such as acting — she appeared in the film *Don Juan DeMarco* with Marlon Brando and Johnny Depp.

In the summer of 1994, Selena made a fateful decision. She hired Yolanda Saldivar to run a new business venture dubbed Selena Etc. Incorporated. In love with fashion and style, Selena had opened a boutique in Corpus Christie and another in San Antonio. The shops carried a line of Selena-brand clothes and jewelry and also offered hairstyling and manicures — they were a kind of one-stop image center for the Tejano girl on the go. Selena Etc. Incorporated was formed to handle the merchandising of Selena products to other stores.

Although Yolanda had proven herself to be a hard worker, she found herself in way over her head. Dealing with people directly was now a big part of her daily business, and her people skills were apparently poor. Designer Martin Gomez, hired by Selena to help produce her clothing line, claimed to have had nothing but problems with Saldivar. "From the beginning there was such tension between Yolanda and myself," he was quoted as saying in the May 1995 issue of *People*. "She was mean, she was manipulative." So much so that Gomez quit in January of 1995. "I told Selena I was scared of Yolanda," he said. "She wouldn't let me talk to Selena anymore. She was very possessive."

Selena didn't confront Yolanda with Gomez's allegations, but then other disturbing reports started filtering in. Around the same time, Abraham began getting complaints from fans who said they had sent in their twenty-two dollar membership dues and never received any of the promotional items that were supposed to come with the membership, such as T-shirts and CDs. He did question Yolanda, but she insisted it was just the result of a bookkeeping error.

When several employees told Selena in early March that they suspected Saldivar of embezzling money from the company she had no choice but to finally confront her friend. It was an ugly scene, during which Saldivar vehemently maintained her innocence and said she could prove it. Weeks went by, but Saldivar failed to present any exonerating documentation.

A few days before the murder, Saldivar claimed to have been kidnapped while in Laredo. She said she had been raped and beaten and that her car had been stolen. In the car had been the documents that proved her innocence. Selena went to the Days Inn motel where Saldivar was staying, and she reportedly insisted on driving Saldivar to a nearby hospital for medical treatment. However, during her examination, Saldivar admitted that her story was a lie. It was at that point, say the friends and family of Selena, that the singer knew she had to sever her ties with Saldivar.

On Thursday, March 30th, Yolanda called Selena and told her she wanted to talk the matter over. She asked the singer to come back to the Days Inn and to come alone. Selena did come — with her husband — but the meeting proved fruitless. The following morning Selena returned to the motel, this time alone, apparently because Yolanda had told her she'd found bank books and checks that proved her innocence. According to eyewitnesses, shortly before noon a screaming Selena burst out of room 158 hysterically screaming for help. *People* quoted a motel maid, who witnessed the murder, as saying, "Yolanda shot her in the back. Yolanda announced, 'You bitch!' and then she turned around."

The bullet from Saldivar's .38-caliber revolver hit Selena in the upper back, but she still managed to make it to the lobby before collapsing. At 11:50, police received a 911 call reporting a shooting at the Days Inn. Selena managed to remain conscious long enough to say that it was Yolanda who had shot her. Paramedics rushed the critically wounded singer to Memorial Medical Center while authorities notified the Quintanilla family. At the hospital, a team of doctors worked to save Selena's life. They gave her five pints of blood, against the wishes of her Jehovah's Witness father. But religious scruples were ultimately meaningless. The bullet had severed an artery, and Selena was pronounced dead at 1:05 P.M.

Police responding to the call surrounded Saldivar in her pickup truck, but she kept them at bay, holding the gun to her head and threatening suicide. According to Corpus Christi Assistant Police Chief Ken Bung, Saldivar "was expressing remorse all through the incident." Finally, after a ten-hour standoff, Saldivar surrendered and was placed under arrest for the murder of Selena Quintanilla Perez.

As word of the shooting spread, Selena's fans reacted with profound shock and then sorrow. Hundreds of grief-stricken fans gathered at the Days Inn, compelled to see the scene of the tragedy for themselves. Across town, others paid silent homage, driving or walking by Selena's modest house. Bouquets of flowers, balloons, and notes of condolence were left against the Perez's chain-link fence.

Selena herself was mourned, and her never-to-be-realized potential was lamented. Latin-music enthusiasts knew that the singer had barely gotten started — she had the talent to go all the way. "This was not some sexy babe groomed by a record company," said respected music critic Enrique Fernandez. "We'll never be sure of how far she could have gone." And Cameron Randle of Arista/Texas told *Entertainment Weekly*'s Robert Seidenberg that "Selena was not merely forging an exceptional career, she was defining a new genre as uniquely American as Delta blues or New Orleans jazz. There's every indication she would have been as enormously popular as Jon Secada and Gloria Estefan. She was about to take center stage as the first Tejano performer to attempt a full-scale crossover, and she was robbed of that opportunity."

Indeed, Selena's crossover album, *Dreaming of You*, would spawn two hit ballads — the title song and "I Could Fall in Love." The fact that these were among the last songs she ever recorded simply added to their poignancy.

When Selena died, she was just two weeks away from her twenty-fourth birthday. Across the country, people tuned in to television newscasts to witness an amazing spectacle: thousands and thousands of Selena fans — as many as fifty thousand, from America, Mexico, and even Canada — converging on Bayfront Plaza Convention Center in Corpus Christi to pay their last respects to the young singer. They placed white long-stemmed roses on her closed coffin; inside, Selena lay clothed in a purple gown, made up the way she would have been for a concert, with bright-red lipstick and freshly painted fingernails. In San Antonio, other unofficial memorials were held, and the local Tejano radio stations ran Selena marathons.

Eventually, Yolanda Saldivar was convicted of murder, although she maintains to this day that she was really just trying to kill herself. She says those who condemn her are jealous of the close relationship she had with Selena. Abraham Quintanilla insists that Saldivar killed his daughter in cold blood because she was afraid that she was about to be revealed as an embezzler. Esmeralda Garza, a woman who knew Saldivar, offered *People* this insight: Saldivar "could have been fired by Selena and gone and gotten her old job back. She was doing well as a nurse. She probably couldn't accept the fact that she wasn't going to be around Selena anymore."

At Saldivar's trial, defense attorney Douglas Tinker argued that his client was so distraught by the accusations that Selena was making against her that she acted to kill herself but accidentally shot Selena instead. The jury didn't buy that scenario, and Saldivar was sentenced to life in prison.

It is one thing to play a long-dead historical figure but quite another to portray a person who is still vivid in the minds of those who knew her. As she immersed herself into the life of Selena, Jennifer Lopez became increasingly aware of the challenge she was facing. She had to capture the essence of what made Selena so well loved. "This movie is the celebration of the life of an amazing person," Jennifer commented. "Selena was someone who had not just tremendous talent but also a beautiful heart, and I think that's what her fans loved most about her. I know her memory's still fresh in their minds, so the most important thing for me is to get it right." But before she could enter Selena's world, she would have to go big-game hunting.

When Will Smith was trying to transform himself from rap-artist-turned-television-star into big-screen-leading-man, he took a look at what were then the biggest all-time Hollywood box-office hits. Scanning the list, what jumped out at him was that, by and large, sci-fi and action-adventure flicks drew the biggest audiences. So Smith started looking for a big, commercial action vehicle. His search led him to star in *Independence Day*, which in turn led him to become one of the business's top dogs.

Jennifer wasn't quite as calculating as Smith in her pursuit of film roles, but she was determined to show that she could handle an array of characters and genres. Signing on to do an action/horror film after completing the heavy, film-noir style *Blood and Wine* seemed to her like a natural career step.

Anaconda reveled in its own B-movie kitschiness. Its star was a forty-foot-long animatronic snake that slithered through the film, wreaking havoc at every turn. As *Entertainment Weekly*'s Lisa Schwarzbaum noted, "With its direct-to-video-type title, it's the kind of retro, eek! eek! production that studios don't often make anymore, now that movies about tornadoes and invasions by aliens have become too expensive to be taken humorously by the companies that foot the bills. The makers of *Anaconda* appear to have no such qualms. Without winking, like *Scream*, at its own provenance, the story is a blurry clone of a clone of *Jaws*, which is to say *Moby Dick*, which is to say the battle between an obsessive loner and his amoral quarry, during which everybody in the neighborhood suffers."

Anaconda's premise is familiar to anyone who's ever seen a nature-vs-civilization-themed scarefest. As a nod to features of yesteryear, director Luis Llosa shot the film in the wide-screen CinemaScope format. The predictable script tells the tale of a young documentary-filmmaking team, led by director Terri Flores — played by Jennifer Lopez — and her crew, which includes the unlikely duo of Eric Stoltz and (yet another rapper-turned-actor) Ice Cube, as scientific advisor Dr. Steven Cale and cameraman Danny Rich, respectively. Jon Voight is the outrageously over-the-top villain, a Paraguayan priest turned serpent-expert-cum-poacher named Paul Sarone. It was as if Voight had studied the overwrought performances of Rod Steiger in *The Amityville Horror* and Jack Nicholson in *The Shining* and then decided to go for even more scenery-chewing gusto.

Flores and her team have gone to the jungle to shoot a movie about the mysterious "people of the mist," an elusive tribe that is said to worship the various deadly snakes that inhabit a certain river area. While searching for the tribe they find Sarone living on a rickety boat, and they take him on board. He immediately sets about terrorizing them all, and he sucks them into serving his great Ahab-esque obsession: finding a legendary forty-foot anaconda. Apparently Sarone has never seen *King Kong*; he is determined to capture the snake alive, take him back to civilization, and reap the rewards. To fuel his quest for fame and fortune, he offers up Flores's team members as live bait — all except for Dr. Cale, who is sidelined early on after a run-in with a particularly nasty insect. Sarone destroys a nest of baby snakes, enraging their monstrous mother. Soon, of course, the hunters become the hunted.

No thriller would be worth its salt without a few crucial instances of bad luck, so the radio stops working, the boat fuel is lost, and one of the team members is badly injured. When its prey is at their most vulnerable, the snake makes its presence known and the body count rapidly rises. In the end, the dreaded anaconda takes its revenge on Sarone by swallowing him whole — then regurgitating him so that everyone can witness his horrible death throes. Then Terri Flores promptly blows him to high rain-forest heaven.

One way in which *Anaconda* does not follow the traditional horror-yarn recipe is that its good guys are people of color — Lopez and Ice Cube are the movie's coheroes. Although he's not a snake lover, the rapper says he was attracted to the film because he found it symbolic. "Political snakes are pretty much the same as the kind of snakes we deal with in this movie. So, I knew what I was going to be dealing with; these snakes are just coming from a different angle."

For Jennifer, starring in an action film was a chance to show off her natural athleticism. "I try to do a lot of my own stunts and everybody says it's stupid, especially actors who have been in the business a long time," she commented. "They say, 'What, are you stupid? That's what a stunt double is for.'" But she brushed aside such concerns. "If I can, if it's not too dangerous, I'll do it. For me, the action stuff in this kind of movie is fun. The action really takes you through it. I got pretty bruised up. But I love action movies. I would be an action star — if I had the opportunity — in a minute. They're tough to do. It's hard on your body to do those things twelve, fourteen hours a day, but I love it. I'm very athletic and agile, too, so that all helps. I don't look stupid doing the moves. You know, some women are not good for that; they're good actresses, but they're not good for the physical stuff. You have to be able to sell that. They have to believe you could actually hold your own."

Later she would tell Dennis Hensley of *Cosmopolitan*, "I'm tough that way. Some actresses are like, 'Get my stunt double, I don't want to have to run.' But I'll do anything. They have pictures of me doing the fittings at night for *Selena* while I was filming *Anaconda*. I was like the Elephant Woman from the hips down. It was a major bruise movie."

But Jennifer headed off to shoot *Anaconda* knowing that the part she was undertaking would be more physically demanding than any she'd tackled before. "When I read the script, I knew what I was getting into," she told Patrick Stoner of *Flicks*. "When we were negotiating my money, actually, I said, 'What? They don't want to give me *that*? Do they know that I'm going to be wet, bloody, tied up . . . ?' I said, 'This is no good. They've got to give me more money.'" While she was aware that "it would be tough from the beginning," she "liked the fact that it would be a strong woman character who is idealistic and has all of this stuff thrown at her, and she rises to the occasion. The fact that we have a woman heroine was very appealing."

Unfortunately, a majority of critics found the film somewhat less than appetizing. "If you like your filmic swill slimy and mean," wrote Adina

Hoffman of the *Jerusalem Post*, "perhaps you'll enjoy *Anaconda*. Otherwise, beware." Jack Garner of Gannett News Service called the movie a "truly inept rip-off" of *Jaws*. "It seems every living thing on the planet, with the possible exception of the butterfly, has been spotlighted in a movie as 'a perfect killing machine,' lurking in the jungle or swamp or desert or ocean. This time, it's the snake's turn. . . . It's the worst thing to happen to a snake since the creature handed Eve an apple."

Entertainment Weekly's Lisa Schwarzbaum gave the film a B, saying, "Acting is almost beside the point in *Anaconda* (except when it comes to Voight, for whom hilarious overacting is exactly the point), and this cast is on a summer-stock level of sophistication. I wish the big-guy anaconda were scarier and that the stalking sequences were more exciting. But a few snazzy high points (one involving that ralph-and-reheat action) are welcome, as is the movie's appropriate ninety-minute length. This isn't brain surgery or even a comic-book superhero we're talking about here; it's a length of tubing."

Mike Clark of *USA Today* was kinder: "This slice of Amazonian cheese . . . is ninety well-photographed minutes of lickety-split camp, a movie far more kindred in spirit to *The Creature from the Black Lagoon* than *Alien* or *Jaws*, though it was actually shot by *Jaws*' Bill Butler."

Not too long ago, a study was released stating that scathing reviews don't have a significant effect on a film's box office. *Anaconda* is a prime example of this phenomenon. During the weekend it opened, in April 1997, it took in $16.6 million, pushing *Liar, Liar* — starring Lopez's old *In Living Color* comrade, Jim Carrey — out of the number-one spot. This was particularly significant, because *Liar, Liar* had scored the biggest March opening ever and had held on to the top spot for three weeks. Part of *Anaconda*'s appeal was that it was the only new special-effects film in current release — the studios were saving their big-budget spectacles for summer. The other plus was the one-two punch of Jennifer Lopez and Ice Cube, two figures who attracted young people. Defying the critical reaction and surpassing even the highest hopes of the studio, *Anaconda* remained a box-office leader for seven weeks.

Suddenly Jennifer was being seen as more than just a talented actress. She was quickly becoming a box-office draw. And if there were any lingering doubts about her rising status within the Hollywood pecking order, she was about to blow them away.

Crossing the Cultural Divide

From the beginning, *Selena* was a high-profile project. As Hollywood looked on, director/screenwriter Gregory Nava set about casting the film's two key roles: Selena and Abraham Quintanilla. In many ways, Selena's relationship with her father had made her who she was, and it became the film's primary source of dramatic conflict.

When the casting call first went out for a young woman to play Selena, Abraham Quintanilla and the other producers announced that they were willing to hire an unknown to play the doomed singer. Hopeful young women from all over the country flooded the production office with their pictures and tapes. But, from the outset, the deck was stacked in Jennifer Lopez's favor; for one thing, Nava was familiar with her work and considered her one of Hollywood's brightest young actresses. "She's beautiful and phenomenally gifted," he has said on more than one occasion. Even so, Lopez still had to beat out the estimated twenty-two thousand other aspiring Selenas who auditioned for the role in various cities — San Antonio, Los Angeles, Miami, and Chicago.

Jennifer Lopez explained that she wasn't immediately captivated by the idea of playing Selena. "I got a call saying that Gregory Nava was going to direct the Selena story," she recalls. "Now, I knew she was about my age and they might be considering me for it. But it wasn't this thing like, 'I have to get this part.'" Then she auditioned. "That's when I realized that there was all the dancing and singing, and then I got really excited about it. We had to do four scenes from the movie, and five minutes of dancing to her numbers for concert scenes."

According to the director, she nailed the audition, during which she was required to perform nine minutes of singing and dancing and read eight pages of the script. "There's no way you can put a character together for an audition," Lopez maintains. "But you can give the idea of whether you have the required charisma and the ability to do it."

She later remarked to Henri Béhar of *Film Scouts*, "A lot of people came out for the auditions who probably looked a lot more like Selena than I do. But I believe they were trying to find somebody who could capture who Selena was, what she was like inside and why she was such a special person. She was happy. She loved life, and she loved what she did. She worked with her family and had great family values. She embraced her culture."

Many established actresses might have taken offense at being asked to audition against unknowns for a role, but Jennifer took it all in stride. "I'm still at the stage of my career where I have to go after things that I want," she said at the time. "It would be stupid not to. Even if I was at the caliber of Sandra Bullock or Michelle Pfeiffer or Julia Roberts, if there was a role I wanted, I'd say, 'Can I come in and read for that?' That's how you get to do the good roles. You can't let it get offered to everyone else before it comes to you."

At the final callbacks, held in Los Angeles, Jennifer came face-to-face with Selena's father. Abraham Quintanilla had final casting approval, which added a surreal dimension to the proceedings. "He was standing in the doorway, and I was overcome by this weird feeling," Jennifer recalls. "I blocked him from my field of vision, and used the uncomfortable feeling of him being there when I talked about him in the scene. The proof is in the pudding, and I knew I had to make good pudding that day."

The amount of control Quintanilla had been given as a first-time producer was almost unheard of in the industry. Aside from being a powerful presence at Jennifer's audition, he had insisted that Hispanic actors were hired and that the production team be primarily Latin as well. He hand-picked Nava to direct and to coproduce the film with Esparza/Katz Productions, headed by Moctezuma Esparza and Bob Katz, who had previously engineered *The Ballad of Gregorio Cortez*.

All of this would trigger accusations that Quintanilla had made sure certain aspects of Selena's life were whitewashed so that he, as the family patriarch, would appear in a more flattering light. But both Nava and Esparza

Lopez with Selena's parents, Marcela and Abraham Quintanilla, 1996
JOE GIRON / CORBIS

denied that Abraham had in any way tried to dictate the creative thrust of the film. "Abraham is the consummate father. He knew if he didn't make this movie, someone would, and it would be exploitive stuff," Nava explained. "He made this movie to preserve his daughter's memory; it's a work of love. He may have been hands-on but he knows when to let people do their job."

The budget for *Selena* was eighteen million dollars — modest by Hollywood standards, but the biggest budget Nava had ever worked with. With money to spend, he was able to recruit an experienced production team, which included cinematographer Edward Lachman and associate producers Nancy De Los Santos and Carolina Caldera. He also had the cash to cast a lineup of equally experienced actors. In addition to Lopez, the roster included another *Mi Familia* alumnus, Constance Marie, as Selena's mother, Marcela; Jon Seda as Chris Perez; Jackie Guerra and Jacob Vargas as Selena's sister and brother, Suzette and A.J.; and Lupe Ontiveros in the thankless role of Yolanda Saldivar. It's an interesting touch that all three members of Selena's band were hired to play themselves: singer/songwriter Pete Astudillo, writer Rick Vela, and keyboard player Art Meza.

Like Jennifer, Jon Seda was of Puerto Rican descent and attracting a lot of attention in Hollywood casting circles. A New Jersey native, Seda had been a Golden Gloves boxer as a youngster, but he left the ring to duke it out in Hollywood instead. He'd starred in NBC's critically acclaimed drama *Homicide: Life on the Streets* as detective Paul Falsone. In addition to doing numerous television guest spots, he had appeared in such films as *12 Monkeys*, *Primal Fear*, *Dear God*, and *Sunchaser*.

Hired to play Abraham Quintanilla was the dean of Latin actors, Edward James Olmos. Many people consider Olmos to be the original trailblazer for Hispanic actors in Hollywood. Far too talented and ambitious to confine himself to playing banditos and drug king pins, Olmos created the role of Lieutenant Castillo on *Miami Vice* and appeared in such films as *Zoot Suit* and *Stand and Deliver*, for which he earned an Academy Award nomination. Olmos, in other words, forced Hollywood to rethink the way it cast Latins.

Nobody seems more surprised at the way his career has evolved than Olmos himself. As a youngster his passion was baseball. When he turned fourteen the muse intervened, and he left the game to concentrate on music — a decision that drove a wedge between himself and his father. "He didn't talk to me for two years. He thought he could shame me and make me feel hurt. He was completely wiped out. People would call and say, 'What happened to your son?'"

But Olmos couldn't be swayed. He took solace in his music. By the time he was seventeen he was making a living at it, and he would later tour with his twelve-piece band. He happened upon acting almost by accident: "I got into acting to find out more about myself. I never thought I'd be able to make any money in this. In fact, I did it for fourteen years for free. I was a singer who got into music and producing and writing songs. That's what I was really driving towards." Olmos took his first acting class in college with an eye to improving his music skills. "And it helped me. I was able to perform better on stage as a singer, better able to relate to people because I was more open. It was almost like psychotherapy for me." Then, as he explained to journalist Luaine Lee, he took a job moving furniture so that he could start making auditions. "It was the only job I could do where I could control the hours. I could tell someone, 'I'll be over at three o'clock in the morning to deliver your armoire.' They'd say, 'At three o'clock?' I'd say, 'For fifteen bucks, you're going to complain?'"

For all the success he has enjoyed over the years, Olmos — who is married to *Sopranos* star Lorraine Bracco — admits that roles are still hard to come by for anyone of Latin descent. "Latinos in Hollywood have been here forever but have never really been able to cross into making American films of Latin themes marketable or profitable," he told writer Cynthia Webb. Still, Olmos remains upbeat. He spends his free time traveling around the country lecturing to school children about the dangers of gangs and violence. "And talking about the diversity we have and the beauty of it," he adds.

Jennifer Lopez couldn't agree with Olmos more. She knew she'd begun to float on rarified Hollywood air. "I'm fortunate because I've built up a little body of work," she acknowledged to Jeffrey Ressner of *Time*. "Still, there aren't a lot of parts for us, and we're not generally considered for other roles that aren't race specific. It's starting to change a little bit, but we're still treated like foreigners who just got here because we're not white." But — "We're as American as they come!"

At the same time, Jennifer continues to maintain that Latins bear some of the responsibility for their own exclusion by not being pushy enough. "African-Americans banded together and said this was something they were going to do, and I think it's something the Latino community has to do, too. We need to realize there is strength in numbers, and if we say we're going to write our own stories and do our own things, then we can force our way in."

On June 18, 1996, Gregory Nava and Abraham Quintanilla held a press conference to present the two actresses who would portray Selena: Becky Lee Meza, an unknown from South Texas, as Selena the child; and Jennifer Lopez as Selena the woman. Nava described the ten-year-old Meza as showing "tremendous promise. Just as Selena's talent and star quality cata-pulted her to the top of the music industry, Becky captivated us. To stand out from such an enormous field shows just how much natural talent and ability she displayed."

Facing the assembled media, Lopez called the movie "a good thing for the Latino community. I want to do a good job and give Selena her justice." She also acknowledged that the project was bound to arouse strong emotions. "It's a very touchy subject. [Selena] didn't pass away very long ago, and she's so fresh in everybody's minds, and that makes it a huge challenge to play her. Even people who didn't remember her now know what she was like, how she acted. They know everything about her. People are going to be looking at me with a critical eye and, definitely, I feel that. But to me, it's a challenge. Actresses are always complaining there are no challenging roles — but here's one of those roles."

Such entertainment-industry press conferences usually have an almost festive atmosphere, but this one was appropriately subdued. As Nava would say on another occasion, "To be perfectly honest, this is a movie that I wish I wasn't making." But he also knew that it was important Selena's story be told, despite the fact that he, and many others involved in the production, had never heard Selena sing prior to signing on to make the movie. "We were proud of her as a Chicana, but we weren't that familiar with her music," admitted Nava. All that quickly changed, however, and the *Selena* production team became determined to present Selena, the artist and the person, to the world. "When this movie is released, I think the Anglo audience is going to discover Selena," producer Bob Katz noted. "And her music is going to be around a long time. The tragedy is they're going to discover her after her death."

What Nava didn't reveal to the press that day was how hard he had fought to get Jennifer cleared for the role. "I won't name names, but Warner Brothers was talking to other types to play Selena," he later confided, pointing out that this wasn't the first time he had gone to bat for Lopez. "When I made *Mi Familia*, the studio, New Line, wanted to cast non-Latinas because there weren't any Latin names. I said no, and I fought hard. It was Jennifer Lopez's first film, Constance Marie's first film. Now everyone's going crazy for these actresses."

To prepare for the role, Jennifer did more than just watch tapes and listen to recordings. She immersed herself in Selena's daily life. She moved in with Selena's sister, Suzette, in Corpus Christi and spent time with the rest of the family as well, especially Marcela. "She told me I was just like Selena," said Lopez — "'You never eat, you don't want to look fat, you never drink enough water! You're just like Selena.'" Jennifer also found out that Selena worried so much "about eating too much and getting fat that she almost passed out."

Lopez grew close to the Quintanillas, who in turn opened their hearts to her and showed her their family photo albums and videotapes. "I watched every piece of videotape I could get," she said, "because you act different in interviews than you are off-screen. I think anyone who does a film like this about a real person, you have to do your homework and find every insight into who she was and what made her tick, and what was the flaw in her personality that led to her death."

Initially, Lopez had intended to talk at length with Selena's husband, Chris Perez, but once she was in Texas she found herself unwilling to intrude on what she perceived to be his continued grief over his wife's death. "He had a great loss and he's still dealing with it," she told *Film Scouts*'s Béhar. "I thought I was a reminder for him and I just didn't want to go there, you see what I mean? I talked more often with Abraham, Marcela, Suzette, the rest of the family and friends. Of course, they have different views. Obviously, she was a wife to one person, a lover, and to Abraham, she was his little girl."

And it was Jennifer's job to blend all that she gleaned into a living on-screen entity. Physical impersonation was not her goal, even those Hollywood makeup wizards were able to mold her features to more closely resemble Selena's. "I wanted to capture her personality," Jennifer insisted, "down to the tiniest details — even the way she rubbed her nose." But the more she got into the role, the more heavily its inherent tragedy weighed on her. "We all felt badly when we first heard Selena died, but now I feel so much closer to it. Even as I'm researching it, I just sit there and cry."

One of Selena's trademarks was her unique sense of style, but it was a far cry from Jennifer's own. Whereas Jennifer, at that point, was partial to "really flowery, pretty dresses" or "Hush Puppies and low-cut pants and short T-shirts," Selena made fashion statements every time she got dressed. Her tight pants and midriff-baring tops expressed her extroverted personality, and walking in Selena's pumps helped Jennifer get the singer's movements down — particularly important in preparing for the film's crucial concerts scenes.

"Our styles are very different," Lopez told Hillary Johnson of *In Style*. "I'm into a more minimalist look. She wore darker makeup than I do. We also have very different taste in clothing — she wore jeweled bras with tight pants, for example, and that's not me. But part of getting into character for me was to look in the mirror and see her face and not my own."

Selena had a beauty — and a body type — not often seen in a main-stream pop star. She wasn't waifish, she was voluptuous and curvy, attributes that are much admired within the Latin culture. So even though Jennifer needed to be in good shape to stand up to the rigors of shooting the film, she also had to be careful not to overdo it. She trained hard, focusing on cardio workouts but curtailing the weight training that would define her arm muscles. "We concentrated on getting into Selena shape, not, say, Angela Bassett shape," she explained to Johnson. "In fact, when I first went in for a fitting the director told me he was concerned, and I thought, 'Oh no. I'm too fat.' Instead he said, 'Selena didn't really have stomach muscles and you might be getting too buff.'"

Selena's level of comfort with who she was touched a nerve in Lopez. "One of the things that made her so popular was that she was always just herself. She didn't try to hide her figure, all that stuff. She was Latin, she had dark hair, and she dyed her hair even blacker than it was. She wore bright red lipstick. It was never a thing with her to say, 'Maybe I won't wear this miniskirt, maybe my butt won't look so big if I wear this instead.' She accentuated what she had. And women look up at her and say, 'My body's just like that. She's showing it, so why should I feel ashamed of it?'" It was an attitude Jennifer herself would come to adopt before long.

Being an actress in Hollywood, Jennifer knew firsthand that a voluptuous woman defied the status quo. "I've always had trouble with wardrobe people! If you watch the films I've been in, you can see what my figure's like. I don't have the typical very straight body. I'm hippy. I have a big butt. It's not like you can hide it. But when I get in with the wardrobe designer, they're thinking, 'Let's see, she's looking a little hippy, she's got a big butt, what should we do? How can we make her hips look smaller? How can we make her look a little slighter?' They're always trying to minimize because we see all those actresses who are so thin and white. Latinas have a certain body type. Even the thin ones, we are curvy. So I'm like, 'This is my shape. This is my body. I don't ever go below 120 pounds.'" In *Selena*, though, Lopez laughs, "it was the other way around: 'How can we shoot her butt so it looks like Selena's?'"

Selena's pride in her body meant that "she wasn't hiding her Latinaness, she was embracing it," Gregory Nava told Mario Tarradell of the *Dallas Morning News*. "Tight pants with the big butt and the whole thing, and people were loving it. All the Anglo guys were saying she's beautiful. There she was with that figure, which is beautiful, but everybody is taught to be ashamed of. Here she was telling people there was no reason to be ashamed. How liberating that is."

While most film productions operate in relative obscurity, the *Selena* cast and crew were constantly reminded that they were dealing with a local legend. "I couldn't go anywhere with Suzette in South Texas without people coming up to her and praying for her and telling her how sorry they were Selena was killed," said Jackie Guerra, who played Suzette Quintanilla. Selena's "like Elvis out there."

Most of the time, film actors work in a creative vacuum. They get no immediate audience feedback and have to wait months before finding out if the viewing public actually liked the work they did. But when Lopez filmed *Selena*'s concert scenes, she understood immediately how addictive performing live in front of thousands of adoring fans can be.

For one scene, Nava assembled over thirty thousand fans in the Houston Astrodome. He wanted to re-create Selena's February 26, 1995 concert, held during the Houston Livestock Show and Rodeo. It was one of the biggest concerts of her career. Lopez, who wasn't sure if Selena's fans would accept her, was about to find out. While some directors staging such a huge scene would have had to resort to tricky camera work to create the illusion of hordes of people, filling the Astrodome for the event proved easy. Observed Jennifer, "Thirty-three thousand people showed up for the *Selena* scene, and they did it for free." This might have soothed her nerves if it weren't for the fact that a Hispanic group had begun complaining that a person of Puerto Rican descent had been hired to portray Selena, who was Mexican American. "I know a few people were protesting, but in Corpus [Christi, Selena's hometown] everyone has been really supportive," Lopez insisted to journalist Bruce Westbrook. Jennifer also mentioned that some members of the Latin media were offended because "I didn't speak very good Spanish — which Selena didn't either! A few days went by then I said, 'This is going to interfere with my performance. I can't get wrapped up in this. I can't read papers. I can't watch news. I have to do this part.' So I went about my work. And there are so many other beautiful things to focus on; Selena did so much in her short life."

Although Jennifer disciplined herself against dwelling on this criticism, this betrayal by the very people who should have been most supportive of her, Nava did admit, "was a little hurtful. They should be celebrating that we have an all-Latino cast and that Jennifer Lopez, one of our own, is becoming a star."

So, when Jennifer stepped onto the stage to begin filming the concert sequences, she had no idea what kind of reception she would receive. Under the circumstances, she was glad she had flown her parents in from the Bronx for the occasion — she needed the moral support. Prior to going on, she expressed her worry that some people would boo her, but her mom insisted that everyone would love her. As usual, mom was right. As soon as Jennifer appeared, a deafening roar rose from the crowd. Most surprising to Lopez was the fact that many were calling out "Jennifer" instead of "Selena."

As she basked in the audience's passionate approval, her worries dissolved. For a full ninety minutes, everyone in the Astrodome stood and cheered Jennifer's every Selena-like move. "It was an incredible rush," she remarked later. "I felt a lot of love from that crowd. It was a week into production, so we hadn't had the time to feel comfortable and ready. And because of the controversy, I was afraid of what to expect. When I got the part I didn't realize how big this woman was and how many fans she had in the Latin press, in the Latin community both in this country and out of this country. I was a little overwhelmed."

In the end, she was glad she hadn't taken the media criticism personally. "Any actress who would have been cast would've gone through the same thing," she told Westbrook. "But [Selena's] fans were great once they saw me perform. I shook some hands, got to know them, and they got to know me. They saw I was a regular person, not somebody out there trying to make them forget Selena. In general, I think the Latin community is pretty happy that the project was made with a Latin writer–director, a Latin actress and an all-Latin cast and crew."

Although the film was intended to be an objective retelling of Selena's life, Nava wanted it to be uplifting. It was crucial that Lopez play her part without a tragic mindset. "One of the things I had to be careful of was that Selena never knew she was going to die," she maintains. "I had to approach it in a very *alive* sense. The way I portrayed her was very, very true to the way she was. She was a jokester."

Also critical to the film was the presentation of Selena's evolution as a musical artist, which paralleled her growing appreciation of her cultural heritage. "The music in the movie was my world, and I wanted it to be what she really did do," Nava said to Tarradell. "We previewed this movie to an all-Anglo audience, and they loved the music in Spanish. To them that was the most unique sound; the other kind of music they had heard before."

Emphasizing the vibrancy of the artist, Nava consciously downplayed her death. The character of Yolanda Saldivar is introduced relatively late in

Lopez showing off her most famous feature, 1997

Lopez at the 1998 Golden Globe Awards

BARRY KING / LIAISON AGENCY

The Puerto Rican Day Parade in New York City, 1999

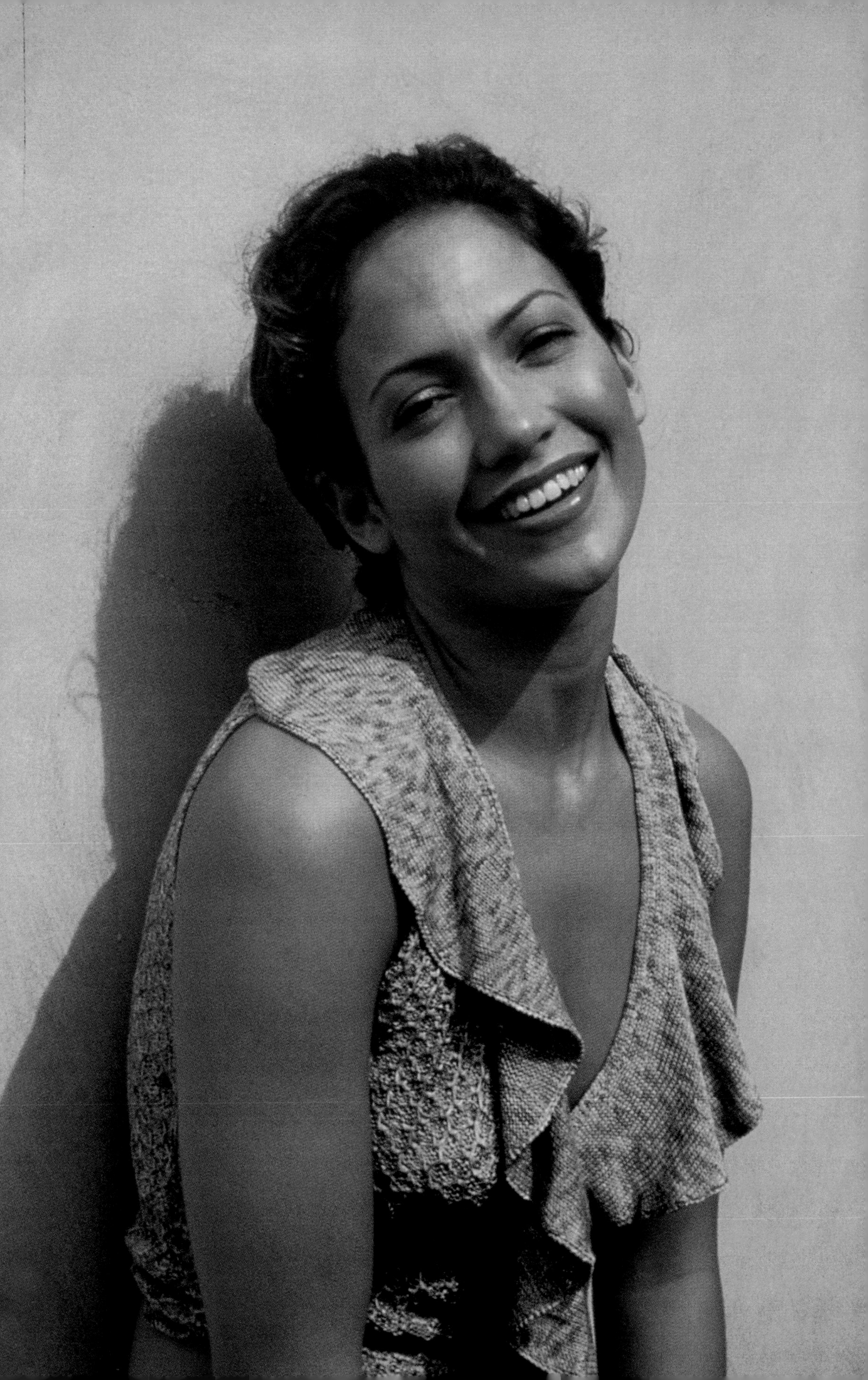

BARRY KING / SHOOTING STAR

Lopez and Sean "Puffy" Combs at the 1999 MTV Video Music Awards

The Dress, 2000 Grammy Awards

Lopez at the 1999 Academy Awards

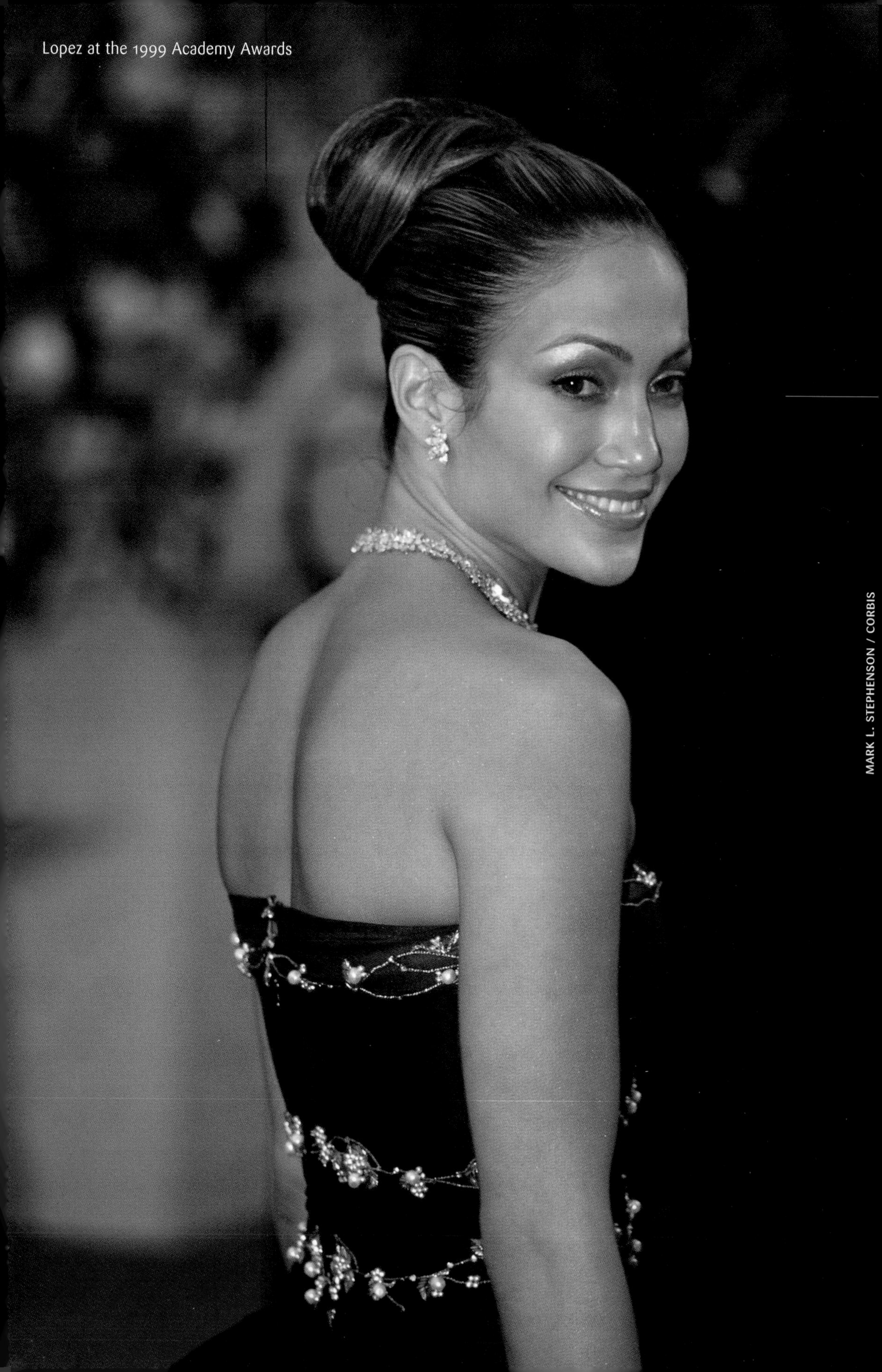

MARK L. STEPHENSON / CORBIS

Striking a pose at the Billboard Music Awards, 1999

the film, and she is allotted surprisingly little screen time. Instead of recreating the shooting, Nava uses the cinematic device of having a radio announcer explain what's happened while the audience sees Selena being put into an ambulance.

"I didn't want to make the movie about Yolanda, I wanted to make the movie about Selena," explains Nava. "I wanted to show enough of Yolanda for you to understand who she was and what she's doing here, but I didn't want to make the movie that focused on her. The psychology of the person who pulls the trigger doesn't interest me. We're always in the head of the person who pulls the trigger. We have to start focusing on the victims of these violent actions. I wanted the last image of the movie to be Selena."

Because of the similarities in their backgrounds and careers, Lopez would sometimes ponder the whimsy of fate. Ever since television actress Rebecca Shaeffer was shot and killed by a deranged fan, celebrities have had no choice but to watch their backs on a daily basis. Jennifer admits that her managers frequently issue safety reminders, but, she says, you can only be so careful: "you can't stop living because of it. You can't think about things like that." Selena wasn't killed by a crazed stalker but by a member of her inner circle, proving to Lopez that, "You just can't tell. You've just got to live your life."

For Jennifer, that meant concentrating on the job at hand, even though the Selena-fixated media continued to stir up more controversy.

A "Vulnerable Powerhouse"

During Selena's brief lifetime, there had been rumblings in certain quarters about Abraham Quintanilla's "stage father" characteristics. After his daughter's death, those rumblings escalated, and some people wondered publicly if Abraham wasn't simply cashing in on his daughter's popularity in an unseemly fashion.

"I didn't do the movie to exploit my daughter," insisted Quintanilla, when speaking to *Time* magazine film critic Richard Corliss. "I did it because there's an insatiable desire from the public to know more about her." That much certainly seemed to be true. Two years after her murder Selena was a hotter property than ever. The question of whether anybody would still care by the time *Selena* was released could be easily answered.

The first in-depth examination of Selena's life was broadcast on the E! Entertainment cable network in July 1996. Marta Tracy, E!'s vice president of programming and development, said, at the time, that what interested the network was the fact that Selena "was really the Latin Madonna. This is the story of a rising star's life, which mysteriously and abruptly ends one day, and it's a loss for not only her family but for her culture, and for the entire country." Such commentary boded well for the reception of the film.

And there were other positive signs of interest. Betty Cortina, associate editor of *People en Espanol*, considered *Selena*, the film, to be a very important project not only because it made Jennifer Lopez the highest-paid Latina actress in history but also because it could well prove the commercial viability of Hispanic productions. "Selena has passed onto this area of martyrs and the world of James Dean and Marilyn Monroe," noted Cortina, "except she's squeaky clean."

Then a book by Univision hostess Maria Celeste Arraras, called *Selena's Secret: The Revealing Story Behind Her Tragic Death*, was published by Simon & Schuster, and suddenly those involved in the film production had real cause for concern. Arraras claimed that Selena's marriage to Chris Perez had been on the rocks at the time of her death (a speculation that had, in fact, hit the rumor mill), and that Selena was ready to give up her singing career to concentrate on her fashion empire. Arraras also wrote that Selena had become romantically involved with a prominent Mexican plastic surgeon she had seen for liposuction treatments.

Naturally, the Quintanilla family denied it all, branding the Arraras book a collection of shameless lies. Others ventured to say that the book was closer to the truth than Abraham would care to admit, lest Selena's golden image be tarnished. What worried Nava and his team was that if *Selena* was seen as an Abraham Quintanilla-manipulated puff piece, its chances for commercial success would be compromised. It began to seem as if the focus was shifting away from the film itself — and Jennifer's dazzling performance in it. Joe Nick Patoski, a *Texas Monthly* writer and author of the acclaimed *Selena: Como la Flor*, told *Time*, "The guy [Abraham Quintanilla] has been so adamant about controlling the spin on this. He's as manipulative as Joe Jackson [Michael Jackson's notorious stage father] ever was."

In the midst of all this, Quintanilla was suing Yolanda Saldivar for "gross negligence" in the shooting of his daughter. Saldivar's attorney, Patrick McGuire, told the press that his client had no money and that he did not know what Abraham Quintanilla was seeking. Those close to the suit, however, indicated that Abraham wanted to ensure that Saldivar would never profit from Selena's death, either through writing a book herself or by selling the rights to her life story.

Still, there was money to be made, and Quintanilla could do little about it when other interests became involved. Heavy prerelease buzz about Jennifer scoring an Oscar nomination had begun. The largely untapped Latin consumer market beckoned, and Banc One Corporation, the nation's tenth-largest bank holding company was happy to respond. The bank put together a million-dollar "product placement" package with *Selena*'s studio, Warner Brothers. These days, it's common for soft-drink makers, clothing designers, and other consumer-product manufacturers to shell out big bucks to television and movie producers to feature their products — the idea is to increase brand-name recognition. Banc One's deal was said to be the first involving a financial institution.

The effect was subtle but unmistakable. Early in the film, Selena performs in a concert hall surrounded by Banc One banners. "It's pure genius," said Roger Blackwell, a marketing consultant and professor at Ohio State University, to Paul Souhrada of the *Dallas Morning News.* "The Latino markets are growing faster than the mass market. This an opportunity for a midwestern bank to gain recognition and generate favorable feelings in areas that it already has a large presence in."

So, as she had throughout her entire career, Lopez involved herself in a project that raised the profile of the Latin community. She'd never intended to become an activist or a crusader, but now that she found herself breaking all the old rules of celebrity advancement, she began to take trailblazing seriously. She maintained her perspective, though, insisting that her precedent-setting salary for *Selena* said more about the industry itself than her own artistic worth. She commented to journalist Virginia Rohan, "It's a weird thing, because I know so many more people who make so much more money than me that it's kind of pathetic that I'm the highest-paid Latina actress. I just feel like Latinos have been underpaid in every way long enough. So I'm happy if I can help further the community in any way."

Although she felt that she was helping, she would soon find out the hard way that it's impossible to please everybody, especially when they're lining up to get a piece of you. Jennifer would find herself caught up in a storm when the plans for *Selena*'s premiere were announced, plans that left many in the Hispanic community feeling hurt and betrayed.

Warner Brothers executives were so pleased with the film's rough cuts that they opted for an earlier release date — March 21. For the most part, major-studio movie premieres occur prior to the general release of the film. They are usually held in New York or Los Angeles, although some are held in both cities. Premieres are generally invitation-only events at which filmmakers and studio executives rub elbows, smooth out any personal conflicts that may have arisen during the making of the movie, and mingle with a select group of guests, including actors, writers, and other notable members of the creative community. After the screening there's a big party where one of two things will happen: either the film's warm reception will be celebrated with happy toasts; or its cool, or tepid, reception will prompt those involved to drown their sorrows. It has been this way in Hollywood for almost as long as there have been movies.

Because of Jennifer's work schedule, the *Selena* premiere was scheduled to take place in Miami, where she was working on location. Perhaps Warner Brothers should have upheld the Los-Angeles-or-New-York-premiere tradition. When Selena's ardent fans in her home state of Texas got wind of the fact that Florida would host the *Selena* festivities they were up in arms. It was as if the Alamo was being attacked all over again. According to Karen Thomas of *USA Today*, these home-state fans felt used and forgotten. "The feeling was, I don't think there's very many Tejanos there," Abel Hernandez, who runs a busy Selena web site, told Thomas.

Studios are always highly sensitive to the mood of prospective ticket buyers, so when the people at Warner Brothers heard unhappy noises coming from Texas they flew into damage-control mode. According to *USA Today*, Nancy De Los Santos of Selena Film Productions announced that "due to overwhelming response and anticipation" by fans, a total of thirteen cities around the country would host gala screenings, including Corpus Christi and San Antonio, the home base of the singer's fan club.

It's tough enough to reassemble a cast — many of whom have gone off to work on other projects — for one screening, but all the *Selena* actors were asked to attend four of the events, those in Washington DC, Los Angeles, Corpus Christi, and San Antonio. Then a selection of actors would appear at the other events, based on their availability. Although Washington DC was hardly a Tejano hotbed, the filmmakers wanted to inject a little politics into the proceedings on behalf of the Latin community; they hoped President Clinton would attend, and he did.

At the Corpus Christie screening, Jennifer Lopez was greeted by two thousand fans. And she knew just what to do, because if there was one thing she learned from Selena it was the importance of treating fans like they matter. Selena "was always very gracious, and always took time to talk to them. She realized that her fans were the most important things. There were a lot of ad-libs in the movie, and one of them was at the Grammy speech when she thanks her fans. It did happen in real life, but that wasn't in the script. I made sure to end the speech with a thank you to her fans. It was a constant thing with her from the time she won her first Tejano music award when she was sixteen years old."

So, in Corpus Christi, Jennifer took the time to address the people who had come out to see her. She told them how hard it was "to be somebody else, somebody who is so beloved. Selena meant a lot of different things to a lot of different people, and I had to do a good job for her fans. I think we pulled it off. By the end of filming, I could look in the mirror and really see her." The question was: would fans and critics see the same thing?

Through *Selena*, the Latin filmmaking community had attracted the mainstream attention that it had long wanted, but the final results were mixed. Overall, Jennifer was singled out for her dazzling performance, while the film itself was taken to task for being a sugarcoated depiction of Selena's life and family.

Jack Matthews of *Newsday* wrote, "Watching the story unfold, knowing that the family had total control over its content, I had the feeling that Nava had put the untouchable elements out of his mind and simply concentrated on what he could do, which was tap into the childlike joy that Selena got from her music and from performing. In fact, if you accept Abraham as approved by Abraham, the moments with the family resemble a Mexican-American *Father Knows Best*. . . . Taking the story as told, *Selena*'s strength is its exaltation of ordinary people undergoing extraordinary success. . . . There are also shots in the final montage of the real Selena in performance, underscoring the brilliance of Lopez's performance."

Dallas Morning News writer Chris Vognar observed that "*Selena* is more schmaltzy than past Nava efforts, full of broad emotional set-ups and success-story clichés that eventually wear a bit thin. But to be fair, the singer still maintains an angelic, larger-than-life aura, greatly enhanced by her tragic death. To expect anything but a cinematic love letter would be ridiculous, and as love letters go, *Selena* hits many of the right marks. . . . *Selena* skips over the teen years. . . . Not to worry; the fast-forward brings us directly to the luminous Jennifer Lopez, a vulnerable powerhouse as the adult Selena. Selena's legend is still quite fresh, and Ms. Lopez is up to the daunting task of bringing her back to life. She doesn't disappoint, playing the budding star as a humbly dynamic figure capable of charming anyone."

Online critic James Berardinelli was also effusive about Lopez's performance: "Nava has brought back much of the cast of *My Family* to star in *Selena*. The two key on-screen contributors to this movie — Jennifer Lopez as Selena and Edward James Olmos as her father, Abraham Quintanilla — had roles in the previous feature. Both are superb choices for their parts here. Olmos breathes life and vitality into Abraham, a man who loves his daughter deeply, wants her to succeed, yet, by his own admission, doesn't know how to let go." Berardinelli goes on to comment that Jennifer is "radiant as the title character, conveying the boundless energy and enthusiasm that exemplified Selena, while effectively copying not only her look, but her mannerisms. I wonder if Selena's family, upon watching this performance, felt an eerie sense of *deja vu*. It's apparent from the clips of the real performer shown at the movie's conclusion that Lopez has done a masterful job of re-creating a personality."

Lisa Schwarzbaum of *Entertainment Weekly* also jumped on the Lopez bandwagon, in spite of her reservations about the film as a whole, which she rated a B minus. "The best thing going for *Selena* is Selena herself, played with verve, heart, and a great deal of grace by the increasingly busy Jennifer Lopez. Picking up the story from adolescence, Lopez blooms as a spirited but wholesome young woman who loves her family, loves her singing, loves her fans, and loves her musician husband enough to defy her father to marry him. . . . When this works — when Lopez is shaking her booty in the star's signature sequined bustiers, doing that thing she did — then *Selena* becomes a nice enough concert film, not unpleasantly gussied up with corny mood shots and dialogue to match. When it doesn't, however — when *Selena* teeters precariously in the direction of hagiography and buckles under the weight of representing all Latinas to all people — then the real young woman herself is hard to find. And it's her unfamiliar audience of potential fans who have to ask, '*Que pasa?*'"

Of course, some critics carry more weight than others, and Roger Ebert is certainly a heavyweight. With his seal of approval a film may draw people who would otherwise give it a miss. While Ebert liked *Selena* — he gave it four stars out of a possible five — he liked Lopez more. "The biographical scenes are inter-cut with a lot of music; Selena's original recordings are used, with Lopez lip-synching and doing a convincing job of being Selena onstage; she has the star presence to look believable in front of one hundred thousand fans in Monterrey, Mexico. Some of the songs build real power, but others are undercut by unnecessary visual gimmicks like Woodstock-style double and triple split screens and cutaways to the moon, roses and other symbols. When Lopez (and Selena) are left alone simply to sing, the results are electrifying. . . . This is the kind of performance that can make a career."

Those who worked with Jennifer agreed. Production designer Cary White called her "impressive." "They were trying different cameras and different film stocks," he told *Vibe* writer Mimi Valdes. "There was a lot of experimentation going on. But with all those songs and lip-syncing, she hit her marks and performed perfectly every time. It was incredible."

And costar Edward James Olmos had this to say about Jennifer: "She has a tremendous amount of glamour, which I haven't seen in an actress for years." Nava summed it up by calling his star "just a complete wow!" When pressed to expand, Nava added, "Casting Jennifer gave me a head start as a director. She already had the heartbeat. Preview audiences love her for the same reason audiences loved Selena. It's because she's wonderful, her talent and humanity shine through, not because she's Latin."

Jennifer didn't appear to be letting all those accolades go to her head. She confessed that her job had been eerily easy. "It just felt like somebody was looking out for me, like it was supposed to be a certain way, and that's the way it came out," she told Virginia Rohan of the *Record*. "It's not so much that you feel a presence, but the movie is all about her, and there's constant reminders of her everywhere" — such as her ubiquitous family, particularly Abraham. "You knew that they're always looking at you and they're saying, 'This is right. This is not right.' But they didn't make me feel bad in any way. They were always very wonderful to me, helpful and caring when they were on the set."

Selena would go on to be the big winner at the 1998 American Latino Media Arts Awards, taking the prize for Best Movie of the Year. Also honored with ALMAS were Lopez, Olmos, and Nava.

Somewhere between the beginning of production and the release of the film, Lopez had entered the ranks of Hollywood's new generation of movie stars and become an icon to the Latin community. According to the editors of *People*'s first Spanish-language issue, which debuted in November 1996, she was among the top-ten hottest Latins in entertainment, along with Antonio Banderas, Gloria Estefan, Jimmy Smits, Luis Miguel, Salma Hayek, Mexican soap stars Francisco Gattorno and Thalia, singer Enrique Iglesias, and talk-show host Christina Saralegui.

While most actors with blossoming careers only have to worry about their own image and how it affects their careers, someone like Jennifer also has to bear the weight of her entire culture on her shoulders. When *Selena* was released she was thrust into the position of role model for young Latins everywhere. "If I would have thought of it in those terms, I probably would not have been able to come to the set every day," she admits. "I really needed to concentrate on the job I had to do, which was making Selena a human being, making people identify with her. I left everything else at the door."

However, later, with a little distance and perspective, Lopez would say, "I feel like there's a pride in the Latin community about the fact that I'm out there. My voice teacher told me he has a few Latin girls that come to him and say, 'We're so proud of her.' That's a beautiful thing for me."

Although of necessity she played Selena as a woman unaware of how little time she had left to live, once filming was done, Jennifer could let go of the illusion and allow herself to feel the tragedy. "I wanted to play her as the vibrant, alive person she was, instead of as a victim," she told Jeffrey Ressner of *Time International*. "I never broke down — until I saw the finished film. Then it just ripped me apart, and I sobbed nonstop for forty minutes."

For his part, Abraham Quintanilla was pleased with the final product, regardless of the fact that many critics had expressed the belief that he had censored the film's content. "It's a very powerful story," he told Mario Tarradell of the *Dallas Morning News*. "I really am happy with this project. It has humor, it has drama, and at the end it has sadness — just like Selena's life."

When *Selena* was released in March 1997, it hit number two, earning eleven million dollars — a third of the box office generated by the Jim Carrey vehicle *Liar, Liar*. *Selena* wasn't a box-office bonanza by anyone's standards — it ultimately grossed fifty-three million in domestic ticket sales and video rentals — but its importance as a breakthrough film made its value more than just monetary. "I do think the argument is over," one of the film's producers, Moctezuma Esparza, said to journalist Lynn Elber. "We've been making the case that Latino films can be successful. *La Bamba* should have closed the door on that argument. I think we finally have."

Gregory Nava added, "I think we're seeing something that everybody knew existed but suddenly made its impact known in the marketplace. There's a lot of Latinos in the United States, and they clearly want to go to the movies and see themselves on screen."

Alex Nogales, director of the National Hispanic Media Coalition, applauded the film, but he didn't necessarily see it as a permanent antidote to the big problem of the underrepresentation of minorities in film. "It isn't about one film. It isn't about one star," he told Elber. "It's about a whole series of things being right . . . so the studios see it in their self-interest to make more films."

But even when a studio does express interest there's always the issue of its executives stacking the deck in order to appeal to the broadest possible audience. Jorge Sanchez, a Mexico City-based producer and distributor of Latin American films, complained to journalist Cynthia Webb that "Even when you speak with possible coproducers, collaborators, or distributors when you have a project in mind, you always find . . . a tendency to want to Americanize a product. But you have to have the intelligence to do it and do it on a level that is still interesting artistically."

Selena boasted "Americanized" production values, but the audiences remained elusive. Its relatively weak showing at the box office indicated that not only was the white audience passing on Jennifer's star-making performance, but a significant percentage of the Latin audience was as well. "If Latinos were to turn out in a big way it's going to open the floodgates," Olmos said to Webb. "I feel that the Latino community has to be responsible for the fact that there are no Latino-themed films." Those floodgates were still shut tight.

While Latin-themed movies continued to be a hard sell, Latin actresses were starting to have a better time of it. Elizabeth Peña, an actress who helped pave the way for Jennifer, pointed out, "what's changing is we're showing more self-respect in the way we handle roles and offers. I've seen actors turn down two-by-four roles or fight to put flesh on it, refusing to play a cartoon character." Jennifer's costar Constance Marie agreed: "I've had arguments with casting directors and turned down roles that reinforce the stereotypes. It's not easy, because I have to pay my rent, but if you're not part of the solution, you're part of the problem."

Change may have been frustratingly slow, but it was real. Gilbert Avila, executive administrator of affirmative action at the Screen Actors Guild, foresaw that as an awareness of cultural diversity was instilled in studio executives by an assortment of determined Latino groups, there would be a new day in Hollywood. Speaking to Eric Guitierrez of *Newsday*, Avila remarked that "Young, talented performers like Cameron Diaz and Jennifer Lopez who are breaking out in non-Latino themed films have done their homework and are now ready to be costars and stars in big-budget films."

If there was a downside for Jennifer to the extended discussion *Selena* generated about Latins in film, it was the danger that, by being held up as the new Latina icon, she would be stereotyped more thoroughly than ever. She continued to repeat that she was proud of her heritage but that she just didn't want to be defined or limited by it. Jennifer wanted to be thought of as an actress, pure and simple. Gregory Nava understood the paradox well. "That whole mentality comes out of a mind-set people have of what it means to be Latino," he told Guitierrez. "We're still very much pigeon-holed as types, as opposed to individual talents. But everything's changing now. These [young Latina] actresses have reached this point, because, like Selena, they don't see the barriers. They are bold, positive and going for it. They're not burdened by the junk us older Latinos are. They won't be type-cast, because they don't see themselves that way."

The basic truth is, however, that Hollywood has always promoted an array of stereotypes, and they die hard. John Wayne became synonymous with the stoic cowboy. Al Pacino was always the actor of choice to play hot-headed Italian types. Characters with breeding and taste have inevitably been portrayed by British actors. It's not so much that Hollywood has ignored Latinas — it's pigeonholed them. Some of the cinema's most glamorous screen sirens have been Hispanic. Back in the 1920s, Delores Del Rio broke the color barrier when she was cast in a number of films with South Pacific settings. In the 1930s, Lupe Vélez became a B-movie queen and created the oversexed, overemotional Latin-spitfire stereotype.

Then for a while it seemed as though the trick to attaining stardom was to blend into the mainstream rather than conforming to one of the narrow ethnic stereotypes it would accommodate. Rita Hayworth in the 1940s and Raquel Welch in the 1970s downplayed their ethnicity and were rewarded accordingly. Today, Latina members of the new generation of stars — such as Sonia Braga, Salma Hayek, and now Jennifer Lopez — would consider it unthinkable to hide their heritage.

Proud of her cultural identity yet unconstrained by it, Jennifer Lopez, coming out of the *Selena* experience, looked to the future. And what she saw, as she put it in November 1996, wasn't "the pinnacle of what I'll reach"; instead it was "this endless hallway."

Jennifer Ties the Knot

While Jennifer was filming *Selena* on location in Texas, her boyfriend, Ojani Noa, frequently joined her. He was on hand for the wrap party in late October 1996. Wrap parties tend to be emotional affairs. Not only is there relief at having completed a period of hard work, but there's also sadness in knowing that the temporary production family is disbanding. At the *Selena* wrap party, that sadness was compounded by the awareness that the woman who had been creatively resurrected for the duration of the project wasn't around anymore.

Even so, the mood was festive at the Hard Rock Cafe in San Antonio as the *Selena* cast and crew drank margaritas and danced to salsa music. Jennifer showed off her dance moves with Ojani. When she finally stopped to take a breather, Ojani grabbed a microphone and walked up to her. Jennifer later told Dennis Hensley of *Cosmopolitan* that she thought her boyfriend was going to "say something about how hard I worked." Instead, he spoke to her in Spanish. "I just want to say one thing: Jennifer, will you marry me?" Lopez was so shocked she burst into tears. A few of the more cautious-minded people in attendance yelled out that perhaps she should think it over, but she had already said yes. "Then he gets down on one knee and puts the ring on my finger. It was very, very romantic."

Jennifer claimed that the reason she didn't have to stop and reflect was that she already had. She'd seemed astonished only because she hadn't known where or when Ojani would pop the question. So confident was Noa, she said, that when they got back from the wrap party, "He picks

Lopez and her former husband, Ojani Noa, 1997

up the calendar and goes, 'We're getting married on such and such date.' That was that."

On one level, it was easy to imagine Jennifer Lopez and Ojani Noa as a happy couple. She maintained she had always gone for Latin guys, and he had classic dark good looks — he'd even done some modeling. At the time, Ojani apparently had some acting ambitions, as well, although Lopez was skeptical. "I'm like, 'After you've seen what I've been through, working nonstop these past six months, you want to be an actor? You retard!' But I don't know, I guess I make it look easy."

The Lopez family welcomed Noa. "I hope their marriage lasts as long as ours," said Jennifer's mom, Lupe. "Thirty-one years." When Jennifer brought Ojani to the Bronx to meet her parents, the two slept in her old bedroom. Then when Jennifer returned home for a Christmas visit, she also brought with her a brand-new, black, four-door Cadillac. Lupe described the scene to Dennis Duggan of *Newsday*. "She blindfolded me and took me out of the house, and when I took off the blindfold there was this beautiful car with a big, red ribbon on it. I don't usually like driving but I like driving this car."

It was important for Jennifer to share her success with her friends and family, partly out of love and partly out of her determination never to forget her roots. As Lupe explained to Duggan, while Jennifer may have taken up residence in Los Angeles, "her heart will always be here in the Bronx."

In fact, Jennifer was seldom in New York *or* L.A. Shortly before the production of *Selena* got underway, it was announced that she had been signed to costar in Oliver Stone's next film, *U-Turn*. At the time of the announcement, Bill Paxton was set to play the drifter who gets involved with a femme fatal (Jennifer) and her husband after his car breaks down in a small desert town. Once again, Lopez would get a salary increase — this time she'd earn a reported two million dollars — and, once again, she would be taking on a role that hadn't been written for an actress of any particular ethnicity (the character was, in fact, an Apache, but the film's producers set up a "color-blind" audition). Actually, Sharon Stone had shown interest in the role — so much interest that Jennifer almost lost the role to her.

When Lopez auditioned for Stone, the Oscar-winning filmmaker was immediately taken with her, but she had little time to get excited at the prospect of working with him because she was heading off to film *Anaconda* and had already begun doing research for *Selena*. When she heard through the Hollywood grapevine that Sharon Stone was actively pursuing the role, Jennifer didn't feel threatened, even though she believed that if the "bankable" blond star wanted it badly enough, the studio would tailor the role to suit her. It had everything to do with timing; as Jennifer remarked, "I was much too busy to care."

However, Sharon Stone and the studio couldn't work out a satisfactory financial arrangement, so the actress eventually bowed out and Oliver Stone asked Jennifer to commit to the project. The irony of Jennifer Lopez being invited to star in an Oliver Stone film was that earlier in her career she'd had a disastrous audition with him and had left feeling deeply insulted. At the time, the director was working on a project about Manuel Noriega — which ultimately never got off the ground — and Jennifer was reading for one of the roles. In the middle of her audition, Stone began walking around the room and rearranging the furniture. She was stunned. "I'm like, 'What is he doing? This is so rude,'" she told Stephen Rebello in *Movieline*. Lopez says that he continued moving furniture until she finished her reading. When the casting director urged Stone to say something, he turned to Jennifer and asked, "Oh — um, OK. So you're a regular on that TV series?" Jennifer gave a curt reply, walked out, and immediately called her manager. She told him that she had never been treated so shabbily and that she would *never* work for Oliver Stone.

But in Hollywood never rarely means never. It's the nature of the business that paths cross at the most unexpected times for the most unexpected reasons. Plus, this year's arrogant top dog can be next year's humbled artist looking to make a comeback. And it's not always professionally expedient to bear grudges.

When Lopez's agents called her about meeting with Stone to discuss his new movie, she reminded them of her unwillingness to work with the man and got off the phone. But when she returned to Hollywood after *Anaconda* wrapped, the director himself called to ask her to come in and read. "I'm one of those people who usually sticks to something I've said," Jennifer told Rebello, "but I got to thinking, 'Well, he called himself and he wants to make amends. I have the upper hand here because I don't care about this movie. I've got *Selena* and I'm getting a million dollars for it.'" The realization that she didn't *need* Stone made it easy for Jennifer to go ahead and take a look at his proposal. Out of this came a vital lesson: "no" is a powerful word, and it's important to get yourself into a position where you can use it.

To her surprise, she and Stone hit it off. "I flirted with him, got tough with him and he just loved it." So much so that when she got home, there was a message from her agent saying that as far as Stone was concerned the role was hers. Stone had also told them that "Jennifer Lopez is like a tall drink of hot cocoa."

Speaking to Rebello, Jennifer recalled that on her first day on the *U-Turn* set, Oliver Stone apologized to her for the whole Sharon Stone situation and assured her that she had always been his first choice; then, said Jennifer, Stone added, "'When a major player calls, you have to play it out.' He was just trying to make me feel better about it, like he wanted me to be really confident, and I thought it was nice of him to care. He's like that. He has a soft, vulnerable side. Oliver is a great guy, highly sexual, and he was so good to me making the movie."

U-Turn is a darkly comic film noir — reminiscent, in spirit, of James M. Cain's *The Postman Always Rings Twice* — which John Ridley adapted from his own novel. In the movie, Jennifer plays an Apache woman living in a small desert town with her husband — not to mention stepfather — played by Nick Nolte. Replacing Bill Paxton as the drifter, Bobby, was Sean Penn. Paxton, who starred in the hit film *Twister*, had bowed out of the project because, reportedly, he'd never "felt comfortable" with the role. As it happened, Stone's first choice for the role of Bobby was Penn, but the actor's schedule had prevented him from signing on. That changed, and he was free to join the cast. Also on board were Billy Bob Thornton as a slightly deranged car mechanic, Claire Danes, and Joaquin Phoenix.

The movie was shot in only forty-two days on a modest twenty-million-dollar budget. It traces the misadventures of Bobby Cooper, a down-on-his-luck gambler, whose car blows a radiator hose in the desert while he is enroute to Los Angeles to clear an overdue debt — he owes thirty thousand dollars to the Russian mob whose henchmen have already cut two of his fingers off. Bobby pulls into Superior, Arizona for what he anticipates will be a quick repair job. It isn't. While waiting for his car, he meets some of the town's residents, such as Grace McKenna and her husband, Jake, played by Lopez and Nolte. After Jake catches Bobby and Grace kissing, he punches Bobby in the face and breaks his nose. Jake then proposes to Bobby that he kill Grace for him; Grace, in turn, also offers to hire Bobby to kill Jake — she'll sweeten the deal by throwing in some steamy sex.

Bobby's dilemma is that he pretty well has to kill *somebody*. Earlier in the film, during a grocery-store robbery, a stray bullet shreds some of the money he's carrying and splatters the rest with human entrails and raw ground beef. He's in sorry shape. He can't even salvage the $150 he needs to get his car back from the town mechanic.

For Oliver Stone, who won Best Director Oscars for two of the three films in his Vietnam trilogy — *Platoon* and *Born on the Fourth of July* (*Platoon* also won Best Picture) — and whose résumé includes *The Doors*, JFK, *Natural Born Killers*, and *Nixon*, this film was a marked change of pace. It was distinguished from Stone's previous productions by its over-the-top black humor and by the fact that it wasn't particularly issue-oriented or political. Stone explained this shift by remarking that he was simply in a mood to "get away and do a genre piece." He also said he liked the idea of using Alfred Hitchcock's style of "telling a story using wit, humor and savagery with good performances" while keeping the audience guessing.

However, one thing *U-Turn* did share with some of Stone's other work — notably *Natural Born Killers* — was violence. Even though *Killers* sparked a debate on violence in film and was attacked for inspiring real-life crimes, the director told *Newsday*'s Gene Seymour that people were missing the point. "Violence is built in all of us, and people keep trying to run away from it. . . . But if violence in a movie comes from a character's action, you must show the consequences of violence. People must realize there are violent consequences to violent action. What is more obscene to me are movies and TV shows where consequences aren't shown, where people just fall dead and that's it. If you're going to deal with violence, you must do it with honesty."

Stone went on to maintain that some aspects of his personal philosophy derived from his practice of meditation and his Buddhist beliefs. These things, he said, brought him "a sense of the wholeness of experience. You see all sides of human nature and accept everything that's within you, the good and the bad. As I said . . . you can't get rid of the violence. And you can't diminish ego. It's much involved in your survival. In Hollywood it's very easy to lose your balance, because the ego is always being nourished out there. You don't exist unless you have an ego, but finding a balance to that is important. That's part of the purpose of meditation."

U-Turn's violence was framed with a dark humor that relied heavily on the skills of the actors Stone had selected to bring his vision to life. In the end, Stone was very pleased with the performances his cast members turned in and with their general level of professionalism. He was particularly complimentary to Penn and Lopez. Jennifer's work ethic blew him away. "She was barefoot for days with fake blood on her," he told *People* magazine. "She's a tough chick." And Stone would later tell *Time International*'s Jeffrey Ressner that Lopez was "striking, strong, and has an extremely enthusiastic attitude. She's there at seven in the morning, ready to rehearse, knows all her lines, and is fearless about doing her own stunts, whether it's climbing a mountain or tussling in a fight scene." Even a couple of years after that, Stone's assessment of Jennifer was still glowing. Speaking to *Talk*'s Bob Morris, he described her as "Sexy, provocative and visually spectacular. She was this tough girl from the streets, a cunning young actress who really wanted to work hard."

As for Sean Penn, Stone considered his comic timing comparable to Buster Keaton's and said the brooding actor reminded him of a folk hero "who walks backwards just to be different." Jennifer herself says she and Penn got along very well. In fact, she became quite smitten with him. He "has a lot of strength," explains Jennifer. "He could tell right away I wasn't intimidated to be there with him and Oliver. Working with Sean and Nick Nolte, too, who is a truly amazing, great actor whom I respect so much — that was top of the line. I could never work with better actors."

The chemistry between herself and Sean Penn was so right, Jennifer confided to *Movieline*'s Stephen Rebello the year after *U-Turn* was released, that had their personal situations been different she might have fallen for him in a big way. "I was engaged when we were shooting *U-Turn*, and one day he said, 'If I weren't married and you weren't engaged, would this have been a very different movie?' And I go, 'Yeah! Very different.'" But, she firmly added, "We both had our own lives, so that made a real difference."

But despite Penn's sex appeal, Lopez was never tempted to cheat on her fiancé: "because I'm a one-man woman. If I'm content in a relationship, I'm fine." She may have had it under control; for Ojani Noa, however, certain aspects of his future wife's job were a little unsettling — love scenes with the likes of Sean Penn, for instance. "You know how Latin men are — very passionate," explained Jennifer. "This is all new to us, so we're both kind of feeling our way through it. We have our rough times, but we love each other."

For the Catholic-raised Lopez, it is important to build trust into a relationship, especially when you're a member of a profession where the temptations can be powerful and daily. She told Anthony Noguera of *FHM* that she believes in fidelity, although she understands how you can become attracted to someone other than the person you're in love with. "It can happen to anyone, no matter how faithful you are," she acknowledged. Then she raised the thorny issue of how fidelity should be defined. "It's difficult to pinpoint exactly when someone is being physically unfaithful. Getting a blowjob or having intercourse or kissing — when are you actually crossing the line? To me, when you're sharing your life with someone and then you start having feelings for someone else, then that's infidelity. I'm faithful."

At that point it was all hypothetical. Jennifer and Ojani's romance was in full bloom and all was right in their world, just as all was right in Jennifer's professional world. Although *U-Turn* turned out to be more of an art-house favorite than a mainstream hit, it was greeted with mostly positive reviews, and some critics expressed their appreciation for the way Stone and his cast had handled the unflinching material. "While its style is unmistakably Stone's . . . *U-Turn* may be best described as intensely nonintellectual," offered Yaak Ngern-maak of the *Nation*. "It's a rude cocktail of violence, passion, gunplay, foreplay, double-crosses, back-stabbing and enough freaky characters to populate the hills of *Deliverance*. And while its humor is writ in blood, it is often very funny. . . . I praise it, expecting the usual assortment of 'Sick Critic' letters." Penn, continued Ngern-maak, "gives a richly dark and comic performance, and with no small arc to his character. . . . For Lopez *U-Turn* marks a nicely contrasting follow-up to her breakout performance in *Selena*. She goes from the angelic Tejano singer to a femme fatale for the ages. . . . Our biggest gripe has to do with Oliver Stone's direction . . . he comes off as Quentin Tarantino trying to do David Lynch. All he succeeds in doing is distracting from the flow of the storyline."

"*U-Turn* becomes a showcase for the filmmaker's terrific arsenal of visual mannerisms and free-association imagery," wrote Janet Maslin of the *New York Times*. "This can indeed be dizzying, what with unexpected angles, sudden shifts in points of view, frequent high-voltage surprises. . . . Indeed, Stone's gleeful experiment is often as liberating for the viewer as it must have been for him. But his film, a long, decadent wallow that cheer-fully includes events like a fight with golf club, ax and Indian spear, does finally prove that it's possible to leap off the deep end even on very dry land."

Although *U-Turn* had been an interesting professional excursion, Jenni-fer was relieved when it was over. She had been working nonstop for over a year, which left her little if any time for a social life, and she longed for some time to just kick back. "I'm a regular girl," she said during one junket. "I like to shop, I like to go to the mall and hang out and get facials, get my nails done and buy shoes. And I've still got a lot of publicity to do over the next few months. Right now, just being at home sounds real nice."

Jennifer had also started to drop hints that she was looking to expand her professional résumé. She wanted it to include "singer." The idea had begun percolating in her mind while she was filming *Selena*; the producers had used Selena's real recordings, even though Jennifer herself could sing the songs. While they were shooting the concert sequences Jennifer was actually singing, not lip-synching, although her voice wasn't being re-corded. The audience had responded directly to the sound of Jennifer's voice, and their cheers had brought home to her just how pleasurable live performance could be. Shortly after *Selena* wrapped, Jennifer remarked that she "was kind of spoiled: the first show I did, thirty-five thousand people show up, and I liked it! That week I told my managers that I want to record something. I've gotta record an album. I love doing it so much. So maybe that's something to work on this year."

Her fiancé was enthusiastic about the idea, too, and he had a sug-gestion to make. "Ojani thinks I should call my album *Melo'o*," she said, explaining, "When you put a lot of sugar in your coffee and its overly sweet, it's called *melo'o*."

But before she could embark on a new career path, Jennifer, then twenty-six, had other commitments to meet — such as getting married. She and Ojani (whose kisses on the back of her neck, she said, gave her goose bumps) had set the date for February 22, 1997, a little over a year after they had first started going out.

Noa and Lopez were married in a Catholic ceremony, before two hun-dred family members and friends, in Miami, at the home of Ojani's friend Joe Fernandez. Fernandez, an American Airlines flight attendant, had known Noa since he had arrived in the United States — he'd come from his native

Lopez and Noa at the *Selena* premiere in Los Angeles, 1997

RUSSELL EINHORN / LIAISON AGENCY

Cuba on a raft five years earlier. Among those who flew in for the event were Gregory Nava, Edward James Olmos, Selena's parents, the Quintanillas, Oliver Stone, and many of Ojani's aunts, uncles, and cousins who came in from the Tampa, Florida area.

Money was not an issue, so Lopez had a wedding planner set up a parquet dance floor at Fernandez's home and hired the seven-piece Latin house band — Norberto and Marisela and the Caribbean Septet — from Larios, the restaurant where Noa worked. And, already schooled in the ways of celebrity, Jennifer hired off-duty police officers to patrol the property's perimeter in order to thwart any paparazzi who might be lurking about.

On the day of the wedding, ensconced in Fernandez's house, Jennifer had her hair done by New York stylist Oscar Blandi, while her sisters and mother were primped by makeup artist Matthew vanLeeuwen. Downstairs, Ojani waited nervously, looking movie-star handsome in his velvet Versace tuxedo. The bride-to-be slid into her ivory Escada dress with a lace train. The ceremony began at three in the afternoon, suddenly — guards be damned — the wily paparazzi could be seen climbing nearby streetlights, desperate to get a photo of the happy couple.

The ceremony was conducted in both Spanish and English, with Bishop Orlando Lima and Father David Dolence presiding. When the bride walked out of the house on the arm of her father, Ojani reportedly burst into tears. Later, as Jennifer danced with her dad, David, Abraham Quintanilla openly wept. Once those tears of joy had been shed, Jennifer made sure that everyone present got into a celebratory groove. She had the band play a merengue, she pulled Olmos to his feet, and the pair swiveled their hips and showed off their impeccable Salsa moves to the delight of on-lookers. Salsa dancing is incredibly sensual when done well. The man leads, but the focus is on the woman, who provides most of the move-ment, via turns and dips. Following the bride's lead, the wedding guests danced late into the night and were still partying when the newlyweds said their goodbyes.

A couple of days later, Jennifer told Marha Frankel of *In Style* that she and Ojani were going to Key West for a weeklong honeymoon. "We are going to sit on the beach and do nothing," said Jennifer. "And we deserve it," said Ojani. Neither of them could have imagined that their fairytale romance would be in ruins barely a year later.

Sexy Cop

Her brief honeymoon over, Lopez went back to work. And she was toting a gun. She'd already done that in *Money Train*, where she'd played second fiddle to Harrelson and Snipes — the difference was that this time she was the leading lady. Jennifer had been chosen to costar in the film *Out of Sight* with George Clooney, a recent Hollywood sensation in his own right. Speaking to Stephen Schaefer of *USA Today*, Lopez joked, "It was a nice change for me. *He* was the sex symbol in the movie."

Clooney had been knocking around Hollywood for a decade when he landed the role of Doctor Doug Ross on the television-ratings phenomenon *ER*. Then his down-to-earth demeanor and his dark, brooding good looks turned him into an overnight heartthrob, and it wasn't long before movie producers began pounding on his door. But — as many television actors who aspire to become film stars have learned — moving from the small screen to the big one is fraught with peril. *Out of Sight* would be Clooney's fifth film, and his box office record had been spotty at best. None of his previous vehicles — *From Dusk till Dawn*, *The Peacemaker*, *One Fine Day*, and *Batman & Robin* — had managed to fulfill the great expectations of his fans and the studio executives involved. His turn as Batman had been the most disappointing of all.

Typically self-deprecating, Clooney remarked, "I think I buried the franchise" — then, more seriously, "The outcome of *Batman* ultimately was disappointing. I don't mean just box-office-wise; I mean as a film. I take responsibility for some of that; I'm playing Batman, so I have got to take some heat for that." He explained that he was doubtful there would be any more sequels, because even though *Batman & Robin* "ended up making money for the studio," the problem was that "the studio is used to making so much money that it can carry them for other bad films or whatever through the summer, and this one didn't do that for them." Speculating that *Out of Sight* would do better, he cracked, "This time I'm not wearing any rubber suit, which I think will be the key."

Out of Sight's director, Steven Soderbergh, felt that it was just a matter of time before Clooney found a role that properly showcased his cinematic talents. "He's ready to happen. He just hasn't gotten the right part yet." According to Clooney, his low standing in the Hollywood pecking order was holding him back, and it would take a bit of luck for him to move up. "I don't know this for a fact, but I'm sure that some of the big guys passed on [*Out of Sight*] along the way. Travolta, I imagine he was offered the script. I'm on that list where about four or five people have to go, 'Nah, I'm too busy.' Then I get it."

Unlike Lopez, Clooney didn't harbor a burning ambition, and he joked that he could imagine the day when his popularity would wane and life would settle into a calm daily rhythm. His attitude was, "If you want to see me on TV or in a movie, you do that. And when you don't, I will go away — which I will eventually. There are very few Paul Newmans in the world. I'm doing dinner theater in about ten years. In the end, I'm going to end up on *Hollywood Squares*."

Because Clooney had already gone through what Jennifer was just beginning to experience — the intense and occasionally uncomfortable glare of media interest — he was in a position to offer her some sage advice on how to cope with the pressures of celebrity. "It's weird," said Clooney, "the work you have to do to stay somewhat normal. Not a day goes by — literally not a day — that there isn't some story about me in some newspaper that's completely wrong. I read I was at Cindy Crawford's wedding, sitting on the beach talking to Richard Gere. I'm reading this in New York, thinking, 'Wow! Was I there?'"

But part of Clooney's coping strategy was not allowing himself to moan too much. "I don't like actors complaining how miserable their life is," he insisted. "I'm very well paid and I love what I do." That said, he might have gone on to tell Lopez that her survival under media scrutiny would depend on her ability to resist provocation. "You can be walking through an airport and here comes some seventeen-year-old with a video camera, and he starts making fun of your female assistant to get a response. He wants me to go, 'Screw you,' and shove him, and that's the clip they'll play over and over."

Clooney was equally frank in outlining the reasons he wanted that lead role in *Out of Sight*. One was that he happened to be a fan of Elmore Leonard, upon whose book the film was based. And Clooney felt that the script, written by Scott Frank, the same writer who adapted *Get Shorty*, did justice to Leonard's unique prose: "Everything except *Get Shorty* and *Jackie Brown* have been really lousy adaptations of Elmore Leonard." Because Leonard's "plots aren't that interesting," Clooney continued, character development is key, and "Scott Frank really understands that."

The *Out of Sight* role also interested Clooney for a more practical reason. He felt that the movie had the potential to fare better than his previous efforts and that it could boost his profile as a film star. He was leaving series television and a movie career seemed very appealing.

Once Clooney was cast as Jack Foley, *Out of Sight*'s hero on the run, it was time to sign his leading lady. To get the role of Federal Marshall Karen Sisco, Jennifer Lopez had to beat out Sandra Bullock. She probably nailed the role when she auditioned with Clooney, reading a scene in which their two characters are locked in a car trunk together. "George and I were in this office and we laid down together on a couch," recalled Lopez. "We did the trunk scene and when we finished, I think I got it. I'll do that kind of stuff to get parts." It also couldn't have hurt that Elmore Leonard himself had commented, "You put Jennifer Lopez in it, that's going to make it sexy."

Once Jennifer lands a role, she works hard to prepare for the demands of her character. Since she would be playing a federal marshal, she decided to spend some time with some real law-enforcement officers. "You learn more by observing people than by asking questions, so I tagged along with these tough-guy cops and just observed — like when a female cop is standing with a male cop, people talk to the male cop. So women find ways to [command] respect. They don't let men one-up them in anything. They banter with them line for line. They shoot with them shot for shot."

During the filming of *Out of Sight*, Lopez and Clooney shared an easy rapport. They would tease each other about their status as movie stars. "George and I would always joke about how the big star gets treated better," says Jennifer. "We were talking about close-ups, and how the star

Lopez and George Clooney at the Venice Film Festival, 1998

is always first, so on the set we were fighting, 'No, no, you go first. No, you go first.' We were both so used to not being first."

Out of Sight proved to be the first film project capable of translating the charm that had made Clooney so popular on ER into a big-screen format. He's irresistible as Foley, a not particularly successful career bankrobber who never carries a weapon. The movie opens with Foley robbing a bank in Florida. After leaving the premises, he calmly gets into his car, only to discover that it won't start, making a getaway impossible. Cut to Foley breaking out of jail with the help of his friend Buddy, played by Ving Rhames, a hapless criminal who has an unfortunate tendency to confess his crimes to his sister, a nun, who promptly turns him in. Foley's prison break is witnessed by Federal Marshal Karen Sisco, so Buddy stuffs her into the trunk of his car, where Foley is already hidden.

The whole movie hinges on making the audience believe that a federal agent could fall for a bank robber. Clooney calls this device "our asteroid hitting the planet. Every movie asks you to take one thing and just accept it." Continues Clooney, "I'm going to have to believe that a meteor is going to hit the earth. Or I have to believe that the lizard is going to walk through New York. You *have* to, or it doesn't work. For this one, it's that a girl, in the time period that we're in a trunk together, is able to at least be open to the idea of falling in love with the guy who's holding her hostage. That's a trick. It wasn't a trick for my character because I'm breaking out of jail and met a nice girl. That's easy for me. It was much tougher for Jennifer. She had all the acting work. We actually reshot [the trunk scene] to get it just right."

After releasing Karen Sisco, Jack Foley heads for Detroit, where he intends to team up with his friends Buddy and Snoopy (Don Cheadle) to rob the home of a former fellow prisoner named Ripley (Albert Brooks), who has unwisely bragged to them about his stash of diamonds. Foley is hoping the score will allow him to retire from crime and stay out of trouble — and jail. As it happens, everywhere Jake turns, Karen is there, and even though she could cost him his freedom, he can't seem to stay away from her. Just as the audience must believe in Karen's attraction to Jake, they must believe in Foley's potentially fatal attraction to her. Clooney explains it by commenting, "He's saying that 'what-if?' thing. Are you gonna act on that? Are you going to let it go? He doesn't think he's ever going to get that again."

Out of Sight's director, Steven Soderbergh, burst onto the scene in 1989 with the riveting, offbeat film *sex, lies and videotape*. It won both the audience award at Sundance and the Palme d'Or at Cannes; made for $1.2 million, the film pulled in thirty million dollars at the box office. Soderbergh was just twenty-six at the time. *Sex, lies and videotape* also helped jump-start the independent film movement, which continues to flourish. Everyone wants to be a part of the Indie film scene right now, says Soderbergh. "It's the new rock stardom. And it's an expensive hobby [that] requires the same amount of discipline and innate talent and savvy that being a successful musician requires." He then adds, "It's harder now than when I came up because there are so many independent films. It's harder to stick out. Then, it felt like you were one of a couple, and now it's just so noisy. It surprises me often the people who end up thinking they should direct movies."

Since that auspicious debut, however, Soderbergh had struggled to duplicate his success, or even come close to it. Prior to *Out of Sight*, he had directed a string of poorly received, low grossing films — *Kafka*, *King of the Hill*, *Underneath*, *Schizopolis*, and *Gray's Anatomy*. In his twenties, he confesses, he suffered from "a bad case" of being "overly serious. And now I feel better at my job than I was."

Soderbergh had fallen so far below the radar screen that many in the industry were surprised when he was awarded a plum assignment like *Out of Sight*. "I'm so lucky," responded Soderbergh. "I mean, I got this job on the heels of five bombs in a row. How many people get that?"

People in the independent film world were surprised that Soderbergh would want to work on a studio-funded film, but the director points out that it isn't a case of selling out or moving beyond his cinematic roots. "I try to encourage people not to be too dogmatic about that stuff because I think it's dumb to keep drawing lines in the sand. Twenty-five years ago, the most interesting filmmakers around were making studio movies, and that was a great period of American film. I think that monopolizing the art-house circuit, while it can be fun and interesting, doesn't have as much impact as getting really interesting filmmakers at the helm of some movies that are getting a big push and having more of an impact. There seems to be this mentality: 'Studio bad, independent good.' Life's not that simple."

Soderbergh says that he simply chooses whichever project seems the most engaging. "*Out of Sight*, like some of the others, just came up," he explains. "Someone at Universal called and said, 'We've got a project here that needs a director and I really think this would be a good studio movie for you because I think you'll be able to do something with it. And what you will do with it will be in line with what we're thinking ought to be done with it.' And he was right. I've never gotten a piece of material from a studio before that I really felt that way about. I guess that's why it took so long because I was just instinctively waiting for the thing that I knew I could do."

That kind of confidence was important, because with a big-budget come big expectations. "I think that's why it was a little scary," Soderbergh admits. "Because we had all the resources to make a good movie and if we didn't it was going to be embarrassing. You don't always feel that way. Normally, all your focus is on trying to fix stuff. This is the first time it felt like there really isn't anything to fix here. I just need to not . . . blow it. That's a different kind of thing."

There were, of course, some major advantages to doing a studio picture. "It was really nice making a movie that I knew was coming out on such and such a date in so many theatres because I'd never done that before," Soderbergh says. "I've never made a movie that had a release date before." Nor had he ever had the opportunity to film anyone with a legendary derrière. When asked by Jeannie Williams of USA Today if he had shot Jennifer in any particular way because she looked so svelte in the film, Soderbergh shook his head. "I just shot her the way I would've shot anybody. She didn't care." When Jennifer heard the question, she laughed. "If they get a butt shot, it's gonna be a wide one; that's just the bottom line!"

Even though Soderbergh was filming a big-budget star vehicle, he didn't stray too far from his own style of movie storytelling. Clooney complimented his director for "having enough confidence in the audience not to explain everything" and for employing his technical skills to advance the emotional content of the story. The scene Clooney singled out was the love scene between Karen and Jack, which he and Jennifer apparently talked about at length. "We said, 'We can't just kiss and take off our clothes. What are we going to do?'" Lopez recalled. "I started to take off my sweater and we figured, so let's do like a strip-poker thing. You start taking off your tie and I take off an earring and he takes off his watch. It becomes a game and by the end the anticipation was too much." The sexual combustion that drove this scene was evident throughout the film, and to the surprise of many, *Out of Sight* became a hit — both critical and popular — when it was released in June of 1998.

"When Quentin Tarantino tried to explore Leonard's characters in his film, *Jackie Brown*, he bumped up against a huge problem: there was nothing to explore," opined John Powers and Terry Gross in a National Public Radio review. "All that film's tenderness and yearning came from Robert Forster and Pam Grier. Which is to say that Leonard is a great, shallow writer, and that's partly why *Out of Sight* is a great summer movie. It doesn't make us confront our psychological demons or paint a portrait of a racist L.A. police force. It creates a world that's brighter, sexier, and more romantic than our own — one where good looking cops and crooks fall in love at first sight and killers do extremely funny things."

In its year-end cinema review, *Entertainment Weekly* noted, "It's not like we have to convince you that getting locked in a trunk with George Clooney was a good thing for Jennifer Lopez. But *Out of Sight* may have been the best thing for both their careers: Her icy hot federal marshal, thrown together with Clooney's bank-robbing misfit, displayed charms beyond the obvious. And like a modern-day Ginger Rogers, the smoldering Lopez finally made classy Clooney sexy on the big screen."

Soderbergh also received kudos for so successfully translating Elmore Leonard from the page to celluloid. "*Out of Sight* may be the first movie that has truly gotten an Elmore Leonard novel on screen, in all its hangdog wit and fractured-jigsaw form. Why has no one succeeded before? The explanation has something to do with the ramshackle off-centeredness of Leonard's plots, but it's also because Leonard, with his ironic embrace of misfits, screw-ups, and losers, is, on some level, deeply in love with failure. Unlike the aggressively broad *Get Shorty* or the overly controlled *Jackie Brown*, *Out of Sight* grasps that a Leonard novel is really a lackadaisical comedy of underworld manners. Whether or not the heroes succeed is virtually a throwaway issue."

Owen Gleiberman of *Entertainment Weekly* saw the film as a turning point in Jennifer's career. "Lopez, for all her Latina-siren voluptuousness, has always projected a contained coolness, and this is the first movie in which it fully works for her. As Sisco is lured into a romance with Foley, you can see her resolve melt in spite of itself. . . . *Out of Sight* is so light it barely stays with you, but it's more fun around the edges than most movies are at their centers."

Minneapolis Star Tribune critic Colin Covert called the movie "A stylish, clever cops-and-crooks yarn with a hot romantic twist: The gorgeous fed and the macho bank robber have a thing for each other. George Clooney and Jennifer Lopez generate sparks in every scene together, and the film is flawlessly cast down to the smallest supporting role. . . . It's rare that a movie gives us one likable, root-for-'em protagonist, let alone two. *Out of Sight* has you hoping that they'll both win. But, of course, they can't. Or can they?" Covert then comments, "Soderbergh expects us to be intelligent, involved viewers. He never shoots a scene in a way that blatantly signals which details are the important ones."

The *Dallas Morning News*, which had followed Jennifer's career closely since *Selena*, announced, "With this film, Ms. Lopez also comes fully into her own. She sizzles as a tough woman with a human side. And she and Mr. Clooney share a chemistry that elevates their romance above the opposites-attract cliché."

In almost every review, the film's supporting actors — Albert Brooks, Don Cheadle, and Ving Rhames — were singled out for their performances, an occurrence that might bruise the egos of certain leading men and women. But Lopez and Clooney were just as supportive of the rest of the team as they were of each other. "The truth is you can't worry about that," Clooney told Margaret McGurk of Gannett News Service. "You just hope everybody does the best they can and they bring the whole project up. I think Steve Zahn steals the whole movie, and that's great. I get to be part of it."

Despite such displays of modesty, however, this film was Clooney and Lopez's star turn, earning them the best reviews to date of their respective careers. Janet Maslin of the *New York Times* wrote, "As directed with terrific panache by Steven Soderbergh, these two sultry stars take an intricate Elmore Leonard crime tale and give it steam heat. . . . The movie benefits from presenting more of an ethnic mix than the book did. The formerly blond and coltish Karen, for instance, now looks like a younger sister to Jackie Brown. Ms. Lopez has her best movie role thus far, and she brings it both seductiveness and grit; if it was hard to imagine a hard-working, pistol-packing bombshell on the page, it couldn't be easier here."

What Lopez appreciated most about the role of Karen Sisco was that Soderbergh had rendered the fact that she's Latin a non-issue. "People get hung up on that stuff, don't they?" Lopez commented to Sarah Gristwood of the *Edmonton Sun*. "It's a thing Steven and I had talked about. He just saw me and he thought I was the best person for the role. I said I didn't think there should be any jokes about cheeky chica or anything referring to the fact that I'm Latin. That's not important for this movie. And he said, 'I absolutely agree.'" She went on to say that, in her experience, Hollywood had become more open-minded when it came to casting. "I'm perceived as an actress who is Latin — not a Latin actress as in one who just does Latin roles. I'm considered for roles that are not Latin, and that's been a big step in the right direction for me. It's something that I've always worked towards, and been conscious of, from the beginning of my career. Faced with two or three projects, I'd often do something that wasn't so stereotypical."

Although *Out of Sight* opened at fourth place on the list of top earners — taking in $12.9 million — it would go on to achieve a modest box-office and video-rental success. It also cemented Jennifer Lopez's bankability.

Dangerous Curves

In March 1997, Jennifer Lopez attended her first Academy Awards ceremony, her husband of one month in tow. Afterwards, she and Ojani headed for Morton's restaurant, where *Vanity Fair* was hosting its now-annual post-Oscar bash. Invitations to this affair are among the most coveted in Hollywood. The fact that Jennifer shared one was further testament to her rising status. Among the *Vanity Fair* invitees were Jim Carrey and then-wife Lauren Holly, Mira Sorvino with soon-to-be-ex steady beau Quentin Tarantino, Ellen DeGeneres (who would, that very night, meet and fall in love with Anne Heche, leading her to come out publicly a few months later), Billy Crystal, Ralph Fiennes, Edward Norton, Nathan Lane, and Tom Cruise and Nicole Kidman. Relatively speaking, Jennifer was sedately dressed, especially when compared to another party guest — Dennis Rodman. But it would be one of the last awards nights where her outfit would go un-noticed.

Two months later, *People* magazine named Jennifer one of its Fifty Most Beautiful People in the World. Interviewed for her profile, Lopez talked about her "curvaceous Latin body," and how she likes to "accentu-ate that." She also maintained that her intensifying celebrity had put a damper on some of her self-pampering activities, such as going to a spa for a massage. "I can't be naked in public," she said, because "I would read in the tabloids about how I have a mole on my back!"

But what Jennifer was actually reading in the tabloids was quite a bit more distressing than reports of minor skin imperfections. In May 1997, just three months after her glamorous wedding, reports began surfacing that her marriage to Noa was as good as over. Speculation began after the two had a loud dispute in a Los Angeles restaurant that ended when Noa stomped out. Lopez's publicist, Karynne Tencer, issued a vehement denial, claiming that the couple was still "madly in love" and that Jennifer had "never been happier." In fact, Tencer revealed, the lovebirds had just given themselves a second wedding, this time in Malibu, which was attended by Jennifer's *Anaconda* costar Eric Stoltz, novelist Jackie Collins, and other friends from the Hollywood community.

Then, in November of 1997, a press release was issued urging entertainment editors and writers to take a close look at a new music video, "Been around the World." "The all-star video epic features Puff Daddy, Mase, Vivica Fox, Quincy Jones, Wyclef Jean, and Jennifer Lopez," the release read. The clip was, according to the release, "Puff Daddy's long awaited video epic," and it was scheduled to premiere on MTV and BET on Monday, November 24; it would also air on Vibe TV on Wednesday, November 26.

The eight-minute video was based on the Arnold Schwarzenegger–Jamie Lee Curtis movie *True Lies*. "The epic tale takes our hero (Puffy) from a suburban home to the desert of a nondescript Middle Eastern country to protect the beautiful princess," played by Jennifer. Featured throughout this "video epic" were limousines and private jets; there were also some exquisite ballroom scenes and a surprise dance sequence performed by Jennifer Lopez and Puff Daddy.

The release went on to cite Puffy's musical achievements, including the fact that his album *No Way Out* had debuted at number one on *Billboard*'s "Top 200 Albums" and "Top R&B Albums" charts, and that he had held the number-one position on *Billboard*'s "Hot Rap Singles" chart for forty-two consecutive weeks.

What the release didn't say was that, while still in his twenties, Combs had become one of the top rap moguls in the music business, controlling an empire worth an estimated $250 million. He had amassed his fortune by making hip-hop safe for mainstream America, with the help of such artists as Mary J. Blige, Jodeci, and the Notorious B.I.G. His own album, *No Way Out*, had sold in excess of six million copies. "He brought a rock and roll edge to hip hop and made it very glamorous," *Vibe* editor-in-chief Emil Wilbekin told *In Style*'s Stephanie Tuck.

Nor was Puffy shy about flaunting his success. He drove a $375,000 powder-blue Bentley and owned a $2.5 million Easthampton, New York, estate. His guests included gangsta rappers as well as Donald Trump and Martha Stewart. He was everything Ojani Noa wasn't: professionally successful, driven, and Jennifer's creative and financial peer. It's not difficult to understand why she would turn to someone like Puff Daddy when she needed a confidant. And, in the beginning, the two insisted that friendship was all their relationship was about.

However, it was becoming noticeable that Lopez usually traveled solo while Ojani busied himself with his new job as manager of the Conga Room, a Los Angeles Latin club that counted among its investors Jimmy Smits, baseball star Bobby Bonilla, comic Paul Rodriguez, and — naturally — Jennifer Lopez. At the club, Noa could meet and greet the top names in Latin music as well as rub elbows with celebrities such as Daisy Fuentes, Leonardo Di Caprio, and Andy Garcia. The celebrity he was married to, however, was preparing to live apart from him. It seemed as though she was sounding the death knell of their union when she commented, "It's tough for me because the men I'm attracted to, for some reason, haven't gotten it together. . . . Ojani is never gonna make as much money as me."

At the March 1998 Oscars, Jennifer, a presenter, showed up without Ojani. She reveled in the perks bestowed upon her for appearing on the awards telecast: not only was she seen by hundreds of millions of people worldwide, but she also got to take home a pile of lavish gifts, including a Baccarat crystal pendant, a bottle of Bulgari's fragrance Black, a gift certificate for Frederic Fekkai's Beaute de Provence Day, a Harry Winston sterling-silver compass, a JBL stereo CD system, a Montblanc Wolfgang Amadeus Mozart pen, a bottle of Mumm's Cordon Rouge champagne, a Steiff teddy bear, and a Tag Heuer watch. Later, at the Miramax post-Oscar party, Jennifer and Puffy got cozy, according to several published reports.

That same month, Sony Music's Work Group, home to Fiona Apple, Jamiroquai, and others, announced that it had signed an exclusive, long-term recording deal with Jennifer Lopez. "It was a no-brainer," recalled Work Group's copresident Jeff Ayeroff to Degen Pener of *Entertainment Weekly*. "I was like, 'I'm a fish. You're a hook.'" Sony Music Entertainment president and chief operating officer Tommy Mottola, who had recently split from his onetime protégée Mariah Carey, said in a press statement, "As great an actress as she is, Jennifer Lopez is also a gifted musical performer. Jennifer is going to surprise a lot of people who have never glimpsed

Lopez and Sean "Puffy" Combs at the Costume
Institute's *Rock Style* exhibit, 2000

this facet of her artistry." In a less guarded moment, Mottola told *People*'s Kyle Smith, "I listened to it and called her. She's not Aretha Franklin, but who is?"

After the announcement, Jennifer turned to Puffy even more, and the music impresario agreed to write a cut for the album she was planning. By May, it had become obvious that their relationship had passed beyond the level of professional friendship. Late in the month, the *New York Post* broke the story that their rumored romance was a fact. According to the paper's gossipy "Page Six" section, Lopez and Combs had spent "two steamy days — and nights" at a hotel in Miami's South Beach. They had been observed by other guests frolicking around the pool, and Jennifer was staying in Puffy's luxury penthouse. "They made absolutely no attempt to be discreet," claimed one source. "They were all over each other and didn't care who saw." Elsewhere it was reported that Combs had hotel security on patrol to make sure nobody snapped any pictures of them. The news was doubly surprising. Jennifer, of course, was married; and Puffy had long been involved with Kim Porter, who had just given birth to their son in April. It had been assumed that Combs and Porter would marry — until Jennifer came along. The *Post* article also indicated that Jennifer's romance with Puffy was an open secret within music-industry circles and that neither seemed particularly interested in hiding their affection for one another.

Lopez's representatives immediately issued a denial, calling the allegations "completely untrue. They are friends." Asked why Jennifer was with Puffy in Miami in the first place, they explained that "she was in town shooting a movie." A month later, all these denials were revealed to have been nothing more than spin control. On *Good Morning America*, gossip columnist Cindy Adams reported that she had spoken in person to Ojani Noa, and Noa had told her that he and Jennifer had indeed split up. But Noa denied that it was Puffy who had stolen Jennifer away, claiming instead that the breakup was "because of her career."

In another wire report, Ojani announced that he and Jennifer had been separated since the beginning of 1998 and had divorced in March. "She wanted the divorce," he said. "She also gave me money and paid for my lawyer. She wanted her career so everything with us went out the window. People change . . . I'm in pain. I loved her a lot."

The catty Cindy Adams also suggested that Jennifer's butt had been re-sculpted: "It's just that she had what she used to call a very well-developed booty, and since I am not exactly derrière-impaired myself, I don't like to say too much, but when she stood sideways, it looked like a Dodge hatchback." Jennifer herself insisted that she was simply getting into better overall shape. Prior to filming *Out of Sight*, she had hired the fitness-training team of Nancy Kennedy and Bobby Strom; the pair whipped her into even better shape through a regimen of weights, boxing, and water aerobics. They also put the five-foot-six, one-hundred-and-twenty-pound Lopez on a high-protein, low-fat diet. "Jen is a great role model," Kennedy told *In Style*. "I'm glad she has gotten publicity for being a voluptuous woman rather than a woman people are whispering about, wondering if she's anorexic."

And Jennifer seemed intent on showing off her toned body whenever possible. At the MTV Movie Awards in June, she wore a relatively demure leather skirt with a very revealing Paco Rabanne halter top, which Degen Pener of *Style* referred to as a "metallic halter-cum-napkin." Although it was June, the evening was cool, prompting Lopez to remark, "I'm very cold but I don't care."

After the award ceremonies over one thousand guests were escorted to the postshow party tent. An array of semiclad female celebrities paraded in — among them Denise Richards, Jennifer Love Hewitt, Carmen Electra, and Courtney Cox. Not everyone approved. Vivica A. Fox, for one, who was dressed in a tasteful pantsuit, told *People* magazine correspondent Jeremy Helligar, "I just want to go up to these girls and say, 'Honey, put your bra on!'" Others, of course, thought this display of near-nudity wasn't necessarily such a bad thing. "It's all about how much your body can handle," designer Marc Bouwer explained to Pener. "Because nobody wants to look at saggy boobs and wrinkled skin. But if you have a great body, why not show it?" Stylist Phillip Bloch had his own take on the fashion statements being made. "These girls are gorgeous. They're young. What's the problem? Although I do suggest that all my clients wear panties."

Although Jennifer may have been a photographer's dream with her scanty outfits, she was starting to run afoul of some of her peers — those who may have thought that she should perhaps wear a new accessory. Like a sock in her mouth. For in the February issue of *Movieline*, Jennifer had given a very lengthy, very straight-from-the-hip interview to Stephen Rebello. In the course of their chat, she managed to diss a number of her peers and a few entertainment heavyweights.

At Rebello's prompting, Lopez delivered her opinion of a number of luminaries. She called Salma Hayek, "a sexy bombshell" stuck playing a certain kind of role while she herself could "do all kinds of different things." Jennifer also implied that Hayek was a liar because she claimed to have been offered the lead in *Selena*; she went on to explain that Columbia executives had given her the choice of *Anaconda* or the Matthew Perry vehicle *Fools Rush In*, and that Hayek had been given the latter only after Lopez chose "the fun B-movie because the *Fools* script wasn't strong enough."

Now Lopez was on a roll. She called Cameron Diaz a "lucky model." When asked about Gwyneth Paltrow, she asked back, "Tell me what she's been in? . . . I heard more about her and Brad Pitt than I ever heard about her work." She called her *U-Turn* costar Claire Danes "a good actress," but added that Danes was starting to do "the same thing with every character she does."

Then Lopez said a few unflattering things about Jack Nicholson and Wesley Snipes, blasted those who issued her paychecks for underpaying her, and professed to be unable to understand why Winona Ryder was so "revered" — "I've never heard anyone in the public or among my friends say, 'Oh, I love her.'" Winding down, Jennifer said that she considered Madonna to be a "great performer" but that her acting skills left a lot to be desired. She also announced that she was tired of hearing people say acting is easy. "Acting is what I do, so I'm harder on people when they say, 'Oh, I can do that — I can act.' I'm like, 'Hey, don't spit on my craft.'"

The fallout from this stream of critical commentary was immediate and predictable. Columnists everywhere took Jennifer to task, including some Latin journalists who had always supported her in the past. Angelo Figueroa, managing editor of the Spanish edition of *People*, ran an item about the furor. "Her publicist called me and said, 'How could you do this to Jennifer Lopez? You're Latino, you're her own people?' I'm, like, 'I am not Jennifer's publicist, I am here to report the news. And if Jennifer Lopez decides to say that Jack Nicholson is a legend in his own mind . . . and that, you know, Gwyneth Paltrow can't act . . . she just really dissed a whole bunch of folks. If she says that, that's news.'"

Some of Lopez's directors tried to come to her aid. Steven Soderbergh announced that he would gladly work with her again, while Gregory Nava said that Jennifer was still mastering a steep learning curve. "It's impossible for people to imagine how overwhelming stardom can be," he told *Entertainment Weekly*'s Pener. "Everybody that this happens to has a period where they have to learn how to deal with it. Jennifer's very level-headed, and she's going to come through all of that with bells on." Casting agent Roger Mussenden also lent a little support: "Jennifer Lopez is a ball buster — outspoken and strong. Some people may not look at that as positive, but I think it is strength in character."

Lopez had tried to defuse the situation by sending letters of apology to those she had publicly insulted, but the damage had been done. Overnight, her image had been tarnished. Terms like "difficult," "self-absorbed," and "diva" started to be bandied about. Some studio flacks started complaining anonymously. One Universal publicist let it be known that nobody could ever be sure that Jennifer would show up where and when she was supposed to. She showed up an hour late for a *Today* interview. A *Newsweek* interview was scrapped after she canceled it three times. Then, in the summer of 1998, she and Karynne Tencer severed their business relationship, and Jennifer was left without a personal mouthpiece. Despite her high profile, she reportedly found it very difficult to find a new publicist right away. Her reputation was undermining her. Putting on a brave face, she said to Pener, "Who cares? I don't. I'm just being who I am. I don't try to be nice. I don't try to be not nice." Lopez was well aware that she was now being called a diva — in the most derisive sense of the word. It was a term she took offense at because she felt "it means that you are mean to people, that you look down on people, and I'm not that type of person."

Perhaps not, but her apparent lack of cooperation and the perception that she had been repeatedly caught telling lies to the media about her relationship with Puffy Combs had dimmed her once-golden glow. As late as October 1998, she was still publicly denying her romantic involvement with Combs. Her association with Combs did nothing to improve her standing within the Hollywood mainstream. Many thought that she was playing with fire. In an interview with Kevin Newman on *Good Morning America*, she responded to a question about her *Out of Sight* character that was obviously about Combs instead. "What is it about bad boys? I don't know, there's something just so attractive about them. I always say that it's like — it's a protection thing. It's, like — it's exciting and fun, because it's dangerous. But also you feel like you're protected. It's, like, you know, little girls

Dancing with Puffy at her birthday party, 1999
FRANK ROSS / CORBIS

looking up to their dad, they feel safe. And there's something about a bad guy that you just feel safe with. I don't know why."

Lopez seemed to be thinking out loud, struggling to explain. Still supposedly speaking about *Out of Sight*, she added, "It's about when you're faced with one of those situations in your life where it just changes; you meet somebody, and it changes everything. . . . And all of a sudden, you're battling, and you have this conflict. . . . You're just rethinking all of the stuff that you've always gone by, all the morals and values you went by your whole life. All of a sudden, everything's just turned around and crazy."

Sean Combs had been spectacularly successful in building himself a career — there was no denying it — but his rapper image made Hollywood movers and mainstream fans alike fairly uncomfortable. The gansta mystique that Puffy Daddy, like so many other hip-hop and rap artists intentionally projected, unsettled them. Combs's tough image was founded on real-life experience. He was born in Harlem. His mother, Janice, was a schoolteacher; his father, Melvin, a drug dealer, was murdered when Sean was only three years old. Janice told Sean and his sister Keisha that their father had died in a car accident.

When Sean was twelve, the family moved to the suburbs, where Sean entered Mount St. Michael's Academy. A good student, Puffy — who had gotten his nickname as a child because of the way he puffed his cheeks in and out when he lost his temper — played football and spent his free time listening to any and every kind of music. While unsure of what he wanted to be in life, he certainly knew what he *didn't* want to be. "I never wanted to be average, just one of the billions," he told *In Style*'s Stephanie Tuck.

When he was seventeen Puffy stumbled upon some old newspaper clippings about his father's shooting. These days Combs describes his father as "a successful street hustler." Still, learning the truth in this way must have had a profound effect on Sean. It did seem to fire his determination to make a success of himself. After high school, he attended Howard University in Washington, DC, but nothing that the school had to offer seemed to interest him. He started dancing in music videos, and he recalls the day he saw some music executives pull up to a location with their expensive suits, expensive cars, and air of importance. "I remember thinking," he told *People*, "I don't know what they do, but I want to do that!"

A short time later Andre Harrell, head of Uptown Records in New York City, recruited Puffy to be an unpaid intern a couple of days a week. Uptown was a four-hour drive from the Howard campus, and the commute was too much. Convinced that the education he wanted couldn't be had at university and anxious to relocate to New York City, Combs quit school to work full time at Uptown. He rapidly became the company's *uber* talent scout. It was Combs who discovered Mary J. Blige, Jodeci, Faith Evans, and Notorious B.I.G. Within two years, he'd risen through the ranks to become vice president. Then, in 1993, Puffy was fired from Uptown for "insubordination." But Puffy didn't need Uptown anymore. He signed a deal with Arista Records CEO Clive Davis to start his own label, Bad Boy Records, worth a reported fifteen million dollars. Notorious B.I.G. had left Uptown and was part of the package. "It was overwhelming, but I had the confidence," Combs later commented.

He told Tuck that "having one hundred percent faith in God" had always gotten him through. "God, for me, is real. He's somebody I can call on." And Puffy has found himself in some unholy situations. In 1991, a concert he cohosted in New York City triggered a stampede that killed nine people, although no charges were brought against him. In 1996, he was convicted of attempted criminal mischief after an altercation with a photographer. He was also charged with assault. Reportedly upset about a music video he'd appeared in, Combs stormed into the Manhattan office of Interscope Records executive Steven Stoute and, along with two bodyguards, allegedly bashed Stoute with a champagne bottle, a chair, and a telephone. The assault charge was dropped after Puffy pleaded guilty to harassment and was ordered to take an anger-management class. "I handled myself inappropriately," he admitted. "I made the wrong decision."

It was widely believed that the rivalry between Combs's Bad Boy label and Suge Knight's Death Row Records — the East Coast-versus-West Coast rap feud — was the impetus behind the still-unsolved murders of Death Row rapper Tupac Shakur and Notorious B.I.G. Shakur died in 1996; and Notorious B.I.G. (real name Christopher Wallace), Combs's best friend and business partner, was gunned down a year later after an L.A. party, which Combs also attended.

Yet Puffy insists that if he has a bad reputation it is the media's fault, calling the rap feud "sensationalized stuff that never happened . . . a bunch of media propaganda." He will admit, however, that he is filled with "drive, determination and passion. I've always been confident, borderline cocky. I had a problem with arrogance, but . . . I'm working on correcting it. I have my good, nice, romantic sides and my ugly, angry sides. . . . I'm a survivor, a champion, a fighter — but a human being too."

Puffy was also, at that point, a potential career liability for Jennifer, who was busy promoting *Out of Sight*. So, on July 1, a news item was planted indicating that their relationship was cooling. In the Hollywood publicity game it is not uncommon for people on all sides of an issue to "leak" information, or misinformation, to columnists or wire services in order to serve their own interests. According to the Lopez item, "people close to Combs" said that although the two remained good friends, the romance part was over. But if Jennifer was at all upset over the alleged breakup, she had shown no signs of it at the *Out of Sight* premiere party the week before.

If the Combs-Lopez romance had really fizzled — and few believed it had — it had done so with admirable congeniality. Not only was Puffy still Jennifer's musical mentor, but he'd also hooked her up with a new manager, Benny Medina. Her split from longtime manager Eric Gold provoked some rancor. Gold told *Talk* magazine's Bob Morris that once Combs had entered Jennifer's life it had become increasingly difficult for him to do his job. "When [Puffy's] around, he's the manager," said Gold. "Whether she takes a movie or not becomes his decision, and when she's with him, she becomes entirely involved. I miss the Jennifer I used to know." But, he added, "she's definitely in love. At the end of the day, she wants to be the mother of his kids."

At one point a rumor circulated that Lopez had signed with Sony because she and Tommy Mottola were having an affair. Such a relationship was not without precedent: Mottola had made Mariah Carey a star and later his wife. But Jennifer dismissed those rumors, and in a *Forbes* interview Benny Medina let it be known that "a powerful record exec had invited [Jennifer] up to visit in his apartment over the July 4 weekend while Combs was at his Hamptons estate entertaining the glittering locals. She was sweating the repercussions of rejecting the mogul." Whether the intent of such a statement was to defuse the Mottola rumor or let the unnamed record-company executive know that Combs and Medina knew what had happened is open to conjecture — although both purposes were ultimately served.

When *Entertainment Weekly* made Lopez its cover girl in October 1998, the revealing photograph generated a barrage of mail from the magazine's readers. Some objected to the risqué nature of the photo. "I don't consider myself a prude, but I had to actually hide your latest issue from my six and eight year olds because of the soft-porn cover," said one reader. Another wrote, "As a Chicana/Latina . . . I find it embarrassing to see one of the few Hispanic movie 'divas' in such a demeaning pose (and lack of clothes)!" However, others applauded Lopez for being a trailblazer "in an industry that elevates the likes of Sharon Stone, Julia Roberts, and Gwyneth Paltrow to superstar status within a minute."

While all of these "superstar" leading ladies had endured their share of media interest in their love lives, none of them had to withstand the kind of scrutiny Lopez was under. Her romance with Combs — were they or weren't they — became such a hot topic of entertainment-media discussion that in November *Newsday*'s Denis Ferrara quoted Jennifer as saying, "I swear to God . . . I've even trained my family not to call me and tell me what the garbage [in the press] is — because unless they're saying you're killing dogs in the stairway for some religious ritual, it's better not to know." Even Lopez had to admit, however, that some of the reports were downright comical, such as the one that she'd insured her posterior for one billion dollars. "When I heard the story, I thought it was very funny," says Lopez.

Speaking to interviewer Brantley Bardin of *Details*, Jennifer attempted to do a little spin control of her own. She flatly denied that she and Puffy were, or had ever been, an item. "Look, Puff and I have hung out and been friends since we did our video, so people started making up all these rumors." When asked directly if she was dating him, Lopez answered "No." But, according to Bardin, her denial wasn't very convincing. Perhaps because everywhere Puffy went, Jennifer seemed to follow. They showed up together in South Beach at a trendy club named Liquid, owned by former Madonna best pal Ingrid Casares. When Combs took to the stage for an impromptu performance, Jennifer was right behind him.

All the while, Jennifer was also putting her celebrity to good use, engaging in activities that failed to excite all those Lopez-watchers in the media. Joining Jon Secada, Jimmy Smits, Carlos Ponce, and Gloria and Emilio Estefan, she helped organize a relief effort for the victims of hurricane Georges, which devastated Puerto Rico, Cuba, and other Caribbean islands in late 1998, killing over three hundred people and leaving thousands more homeless. In addition to donating fifty thousand dollars of their own money, the Estefans mounted a telethon to help raise more funds, and Jennifer was among the celebrities who participated.

It must have frustrated Jennifer that while the media practically ignored her involvement in pursuits such as these, journalists remained enthralled by her relationship with Combs and her generous posterior. In its December issue *Details* named Jennifer Lopez the sexiest woman of the year and mentioned her highly publicized behind. Jennifer responded with patience. "I think it started with *Selena* and all those tight pants. But you know, I don't have to be a size two to be sexy," she told the magazine. "I guess not being ashamed of something like that, which is uncharacteristic of this society, made it become a focal point."

It just wouldn't go away. Other celebrities began to make snarky remarks on the record about that famous butt. Cindy Crawford actually remarked to *Self* magazine, "I don't know if I would have the guts to walk around with that butt. . . . Is it cultural, or what was she given in self-confidence that I wasn't?" Crawford apparently crossed a line, because when *People* ran an item about her statement it elicited reader responses like these: "Her comment on Jennifer Lopez's derriere was ignorant and spiteful. Jennifer has an incredible figure — one that I'm sure many women would not mind having"; "Cindy, put on a few pounds and maybe you could have a figure befitting a woman rather than a twelve-year-old boy"; "Cindy Crawford's statement about Jennifer Lopez was borderline racist. . . . More women should be like Miss Lopez. She has a full, beautiful figure that she doesn't hide or make excuses for — she celebrates it!"

This kind of support was welcome, but there was no denying that 1998 had been a particularly stressful year for Lopez. Insult was added to injury at the second-annual Chuy Awards, which had been created to honor the best — and worst — in the world of Latin entertainment. A year earlier, everyone had been singing Jennifer's praises for her work in *Selena*, but this year she was given a swift kick in her generous butt. The Chuy for the Worst Talk Show Guest Pushing a New Movie went to Jennifer Lopez for her less-than-scintillating efforts on behalf of *Out of Sight*.

Commenting on the characters she tended to play Jennifer once said, "I don't think of them as strong women. I like characters that are really part of the story as opposed to window dressing — but I think the interesting thing is that they are real people. Nobody walks around being strong all the time." There were times during 1998 that Jennifer could have crumbled, but she didn't. Instead, she learned some hard lessons, the first being, "I absolutely watch what I say more. I make my point, and I don't say much else." She also learned that it would be wise to reach beyond her goal of being a big movie star and explore some new terrain. "I want everything. I want family. I want to do good work. I want love. I want to be comfortable," she confided. "I think of people like Cher and Bette Midler and Diana Ross and Barbra Streisand. That's always been the kind of career I'd hoped to have. I want it all." But she'd get more than she bargained for in the process of attaining it.

Love Songs

A sure sign that someone has achieved A-list movie-star status is when they are invited to lend their voice to a big-budget animated feature. Ever since Disney started delighting — and in some cases terrorizing — children with his innovative feature-length cartoons, generations of actors have grown up mesmerized by animation with its boundless imaginative potential. Most jump at the opportunity to be a voice character in a movie; they see it as something they will be able to show to their kids and grandkids with pride.

Antz was the first animated effort to come out of DreamWorks SGK, a company founded by Stephen Spielberg, music mogul David Geffen, and embittered former Disney executive Jeffrey Katzenberg. Among the voice talent assembled for the film were Woody Allen, Sharon Stone, Sylvester Stallone, Gene Hackman, Dan Aykroyd, Jane Curtin, Danny Glover, and Jennifer Lopez. The story focused on a worker ant named Z (Woody Allen) whose function in life is to be a "soil relocation engineer" — in other words, to dig new tunnels and move dirt. The meaningless nature of his existence makes Z feel insignificant, a concern he shares with his psychiatrist. His ant friends, including a soldier named Weaver (Stallone) and a fellow worker ant called Azteca (Lopez), try to make Z understand that his significance lies in his contribution to the colony as a whole. Of course none of this makes Z feel any better.

Meanwhile, General Mandible (Gene Hackman) and the winged Colonel Cutter (Christopher Walken) are plotting a coup. Their plan is to kill all of the workers, whom they consider the weak part of the colony, as well as the queen, and create an all-soldier colony. Aware that after the coup they will still need to reproduce, Mandible manipulates the queen into agreeing to let him marry her daughter, Princess Vala (Sharon Stone). Vala is miserable at the prospect of a loveless arranged marriage.

In a show of independence, she sneaks out of the royal lodgings and makes her way to the workers' bar, where she ends up dancing with Z. Naturally, he falls head-over-heels in love with her. The rest of the film follows Z's attempt to win Vala's love while saving her and the colony from the evil General Mandible.

Voice casting is an interesting exercise. In an animated film, an actor's physical attributes are meaningless and his or her ability to convey personality through voice counts for everything. *Antz* codirector Eric Darnell said that Jennifer was perfect for Azteca because, "She's got this great combination of control and invulnerability — she came from the Bronx and had to hold her own there — and also a certain sort of sensualness that's hard to come by."

Darnell also claimed that getting big names to work on the project wasn't as important to the film's box-office success as people might imagine. "Sure, we get a little press for getting Woody Allen, Gene Hackman and Sharon Stone to do your characters. And it's great to animate these performances, no question about it. But once you get past the recognition, it's the characters that have to keep you interested and involved." And to those who might think supplying the voice for an animated character is an easy way to pick up a fat paycheck, Jeffrey Katzenberg had this to say: it's the "most demanding, absolutely hardest job" an actor can do.

Sandra Bullock, who was the voice of Moses's sister Miriam in the DreamWorks production of *The Prince of Egypt*, told Gene Seymour of *Newsday* that being alone in a sound booth with no other actors to play off is a little intimidating: "I relate better to people physically, rather than verbally. And for the couple of days I did the recording, I felt so isolated. I've never had this experience before." Anne Bancroft, who was the voice of the queen in *Antz*, called the experience "like being in space. You're acting to this piece of paper in front of you. You have to become a storyteller yourself, because you're required to use your imagination" — to visualize.

But if there was one thing that Jennifer Lopez excelled at it was visualization. As a child she had seen herself as a dancer, and she became one; as a teenager she imagined herself on the big screen, and she pulled it off;

Performing at the Billboard Music Awards, 1999

now, she was beginning to see herself as a pop star, and she was determined to realize that dream too, despite the strong possibility of failure. Nobody had managed it since Bette Midler — an A-list film actress who could still score a Top 40 hit. But Midler had become famous as a singer first, and her hit songs generally came from movie soundtracks. Lopez intended to establish herself as a singer independent from her work in the movies. When it was pointed out that she was taking a big risk and would perhaps lose some of her hard-earned professional credibility, she was unswayed. "How can I live my life in fear like that? The winners take risks. That's the only way to be. I would hate to be fifty years old and think I should have done that back then."

Jennifer could not have picked a better time for a foray into the music world. If there was a zeitgeist, it had a Latin beat. Suddenly the entire music world was embracing all things Latin. "I have no crystal ball, but my gut tells me that Latin music can be the next big reservoir of talent for mainstream superstars," said Tommy Mottola, who was so convinced that Latin music would be the next big thing, sources say, that he earmarked upwards of ten million dollars to promote Ricky Martin's English-language album and even more to hire top-notch producers like Puff Daddy and David Foster, entrusting them with the task of guiding Sony's Latin division down the same path country and hip-hop had taken.

To see the wisdom of this, just consider the numbers: more than four hundred million people worldwide identify Spanish as their first language. In America alone, there are over thirty million people of Hispanic descent — well over ten percent of the total population. Cable tapped into this market years ago; MTV has been expanding its MTV Latin America Central and South America since the early 1990s. The network also broadcasts *MTV en Espanol* in the United States, programming aimed at a young, bilingual group of consumers who have been largely overlooked.

The new wave of Latin talent coming into our living rooms doesn't create the rhythms for your father's lambada or your brother's macarena — there's nothing gimmicky about it. Latin sounds are as old as music itself. Prior to Martin, the most successful crossover Latin artist was Gloria Estefan; she was the first to tap into the staggering potential of Latin music. But the success of Estefan and her husband, Emilio, wasn't fueled entirely by their Latin followers. Through music, they reached across the cultural divide and gathered together non-Hispanics by the arena-full, which is one reason why sales of Latin music rose twenty-five percent in 1997. Like Ricky Martin, the Estefans won people over through hard work and infectious rhythms. They began humbly in the 1970s as the Miami Sound Machine. They scraped by until Sony offered to sign them in 1981. They hit in Latin America first, with two Spanish-language albums, then they broke through in America with the song "Conga."

Other acts soon followed the energetic lead of the Miami Sound Machine, blending Latin rhythms with dance beats and appealing to Hispanics and Anglos alike. Believing that they'd found the right formula, the Estefans put their life savings towards producing their first English-language album for Sony, *Primitive Love*. Their gamble paid off when it became the first in a string of multiplatinum albums. But the Estefans did more than just ride the wave of their own success. They set out to nurture, develop, and promote other Latin artists, such as John Secada, who began as a songwriter for the Estefan's record company. Under their guidance, Secada also became a multiplatinum-album act.

The Estefans now employ over two dozen songwriters and almost as many musicians and producers at their record company and studio. They're not afraid to extend their talent search across the border, either. They have worked with such artists as Thalia, a well-known Mexican *novella* star and singer, and Alejandro Fernandez, one of the country's most famous mariachi performers. The Estefan's music machine has made them multi-millionaires — their net worth is over two hundred million dollars.

Which is why, throughout the recording industry, labels are anxious to sign Latin artists. And those artists have become ubiquitous. In the middle of Hollywood, a huge headshot of Enrique Iglesias peered for awhile from a billboard promoting the local Spanish-language radio station. Luis Miguel, another Latin pop singer, sold more than twelve million copies of the first two albums in his Warner Music *Romance* trilogy.

Another gauge of Latin music's popularity is its dance-club domination, not only in America but also around the world. While nobody would be surprised to learn that many clubs in L.A. and Miami now favor the Latin sound, it does come as a bit of a surprise that it's all the rage in places like London, as well.

When Jennifer first decided to pursue a music career, she originally planned to do it in Spanish. "I did a demo in Spanish after *Selena* and submitted it to the Work label," she told Christopher Farley of *Time*. "They said, 'We like it, but we want you to do it in English.'" So although Lopez wasn't a Spanish-language performer trying to cross over, and even though her sounds were decidedly mainstream pop, she clearly benefited from the surge of interest in Latin artists. It didn't hurt, either, that she was constantly being singled out for one honor or another. Once again, in 1999, *People* magazine inscribed her on their 50 Most Beautiful People list. This time, Jennifer told her *People* interviewer that to her beauty is an aspect of self-assurance, and credited her parents for instilling that in her. "Every time I call, my dad says, 'Hi, gorgeous.' That makes me feel beautiful." She added that she was happy to be a poster girl for the voluptuous. "For so long it was just skinny, skinny, skinny. I'm glad to contribute to the self-esteem of others."

Originally, Lopez was going to call her album *Gypsy*, a reference to her days as a dancer. In the end, though, she chose to pay homage to the train that carried her into New York to chase her dreams — she titled the album *On the 6*. Her music, she said, is a "kind of a hybrid — the music somebody like me would like, who grew up in the Bronx, of Latin descent but a very American family." Sony backed up the project with some serious and expensive talent: Puffy Combs and Emilio Estefan — who had guided his wife, Gloria, to the top of the charts so many times — were two of Jennifer's producers.

As the album's release date neared, Sony got the publicity machine going full throttle. They arranged for Jennifer Lopez and Ricky Martin to do a photo shoot together, hoping that some of the frenzy surrounding Martin's debut English-language album would rub off on Lopez. Puffy accompanied Jennifer to the Manhattan studio where the shoot took place, and he watched as she posed seductively with the handsome young performer whose album had debuted at number one on the *Billboard* chart. Jennifer's own album was due to be released the following week. She told Veronica Chambers and John Leland of *Newsweek* that "It's always a good time to be Latin," but now, she added, "the world is starting to see what it's like to grow up in a Latin family: the flavor and the culture and the passion and the music. We're a very passionate people." Despite remarks such as these, however, *On the 6* was less about passion and more about safe commercialism. Production values were slick, and the cuts contained carefully measured amounts of R&B and Latin rhythms. Unlike Martin's last

Performing at the VH1–Vogue Fashion Awards, 1999
© REUTERS NEWMEDIA INC. / CORBIS

Spanish-language album, *Vuelve*, which had won him a Grammy, *On the 6* was no groundbreaker. It was safe.

In a *Vibe* interview with Dream Hampton, Jennifer declared, "I can't try to be Whitney or Faith. I do something different. I have something else to offer to anybody who'll want to, you know, fucking get down." In the same interview, Big Pun, who worked with Jennifer on an album track called "Feeling So Good," which was produced by Puffy, said that Jennifer "represents all the things that [Latinos] are: beautiful, voluptuous, intelligent, proud."

One interesting side note about Jennifer Lopez and Ricky Martin is that at the time of their photo shoot, Lopez was in negotiations to make a new film version of the classic Broadway musical *West Side Story*. "Natalie Wood needed makeup to play a Puerto Rican girl in the original [film version]," she told *London Free Press* interviewer Louis Hobson. "I have been fighting to play characters written white, but this is one time I will proudly play ethnic. I long for the day when Hollywood will truly be color blind." Martin was also approached about the project, but, unlike Lopez, who had a sentimental place in her heart for the musical, Martin showed no interest in updating the classic, telling *Newsweek*, "It would represent gangs and stereotypes about my culture."

So, if the *West Side Story* project was to proceed, it would have to do so without the king of Latin heartthrobs. And of more immediate concern to Lopez than these project negotiations was her album. At least on the surface, she could not have asked for a more auspicious debut. *On the 6* made history by hitting number one on the Hot 100, Hot 100 Singles Sales, and R&B Singles Sales charts simultaneously; and "If You Had My Love," the album's first single, headed to the top of the pop charts. Lopez, who cowrote three of the songs on the album, chatted about her craft with *In Style*: "You have to have heightened emotions. If you're really happy, angry, depressed or in love, you can write a good song."

And, apparently, Lopez was feeling ecstatic. Her album, which would eventually go on to achieve double-platinum status, was being promoted with all the ferocity Sony could muster, and she was the latest darling of the musical world. In May, she and singer Marc Anthony — with whom she'd sung a ballad on the album — appeared together at the record release party for *On the 6* at the Manhattan nightclub Float. The *New York Daily News* implied that Anthony and Lopez were now a romantic item, although the reporter acknowledged that Jennifer had, in fact, spent most of the evening dancing with a variety of partners, including model Taye Diggs and baseball star Derek Jeter.

The hype onslaught that Sony had orchestrated for *On the 6* seemed to counterbalance the generally poor reviews the record received. In a lengthy critique, *Entertainment Weekly* gave it a C grade. "Despite an all-star cast, Jennifer Lopez's singing isn't out-of-sight," wrote David Browne. He also pointed out that despite all those high-profile producers who had been brought into the project — "all recruited to add heft to Lopez's career

Lopez at the party to promote her album *On the 6*, 1999

makeover" — the problem was that "as soon as Lopez opens her mouth . . . all this advance work falls by the wayside."

Her singing voice, observed Browne, is "higher and thinner than expected — not embarrassing, but sadly ordinary." He also considered the album's ballads "prissy" and the dance cuts "tame." As far as he was concerned, only "Waiting for Tonight" stood out — a cut "worthy of a dance-floor diva." Browne concluded by predicting that twenty years down the road "this album will be part of someone's doctoral thesis on the dangers of crossover. For all the wads of money spent on her fledging musical career, Lopez comes across as little more than a Mild Spice Girl."

Wall of Sound reviewer Daniel Durchholz echoed Browne. "Producers and guest stars can only do so much, and there are problems with the material and with Lopez's own performances that make *On the 6* an ultimately disappointing effort. In the first place, though it's never wincingly bad, her voice is weak." Durchholz also took issue with the production of the songs pointing to the spoken-word section of "Should've Never," "where she whispers and coos in Spanish like a Puerto Rican reincarnation of Claudine Longet. It's supposed to be sexy, of course, but Latin pop is full of such overwrought moments."

Ben Werner of the *Orange County Register* had some kinder words for Jennifer herself, noting, "Sure enough, Lopez can sing — and well, actually there is a surprising tenderness to her sometimes-sultry coo"; but he went on to skewer the song lyrics, calling them "horrendous. Take this seventh-grade passage, for instance, from 'Talk about Us': 'I saw you and fell in love, too / You saw me and fell in love, too / You and me, we fell in love with each other / Last night' Wow. Heavy."

In his overview of the new crop of Latin performers, Mike Usinger of the web site Infoculture was hard on Lopez. "As laughable as the ballads are, the rest of *On the 6* isn't much better. Instead of lively salsa fusion, we get shockingly sub-par dance tracks. Forget fired-up flamenco pop, the best we get here is the white-washed R&B of 'If You Had My Love.' Simply because she's Latin, Lopez is going to end up one of the most overplayed artists of the summer. Yes, she may look great, but I want a little substance with my sex appeal. And if I'm going to buy into the Latin craze I want a full-blown fiesta. Quite frankly, I don't think Lopez would know a piña colada from a piñata."

Entertainment Weekly's Betty Cortina picked up that "she may be Latin but her music isn't" theme, applying it to Martin, as well. "While Martin and Lopez are bona fide Latinos (he from the balmy beaches of Puerto Rico, she from the balmy borough of the Bronx, N.Y.), their current hit albums are unapologetic pop. Save for a brassy horn riff here and a Spanish-guitar fill there, the music's as Latin as, say, George Michael or Janet Jackson."

In fact, a number of other artists were also being accused of jumping on the Latin bandwagon, including Puffy, who included a Spanish song on one of his own albums. Corey Takahashi of *Entertainment Weekly* reported that Combs's representatives had insisted the track was Puffy's gesture of appreciation for his Latino fans; then Takahashi quoted one Latin-music insider's response to it: "That thing was horrible. The translation, the pronunciation, the enunciation — everything you can think of."

Through all of this, as the critics complained and *On the 6* flew off record-store shelves, Jennifer and Puffy hung together — despite some anonymous-source reports in New York gossip columns that Jennifer and Marc Anthony were hot and heavy. Finally, in the summer of 1999, *Star* magazine reported that Lopez and Combs had finally gone public with their romance, at her twenty-ninth birthday party held on July 24 at New York City's Halo Club. Guests at the star-studded celebration — including Leonardo DiCaprio, Derek Jeter, Donald Trump, Vivica A. Fox, Stephen Baldwin, and Queen Latifah — ate bright-pink birthday cake and watched Jennifer and Puffy kiss and cuddle in a corner.

But while their private lives may have been blissful, Combs's accelerating career was hitting some unexpected bumps. A number of artists on his label were upset that Combs only seemed interested in promoting his own albums, leaving them to simmer on the back burner. "I applaud Puffy's success," Faith Evans told Johnnie Roberts of *Newsweek*. "But I do feel it took away a lot of attention in terms of work and thought put into other artists. His time availability isn't the same. A lot of artists aren't happy." In fact, one prominent group, the top-selling rap outfit called The Lox, defected and signed with Interscope, citing a "combination of irreconcilable differences."

Puffy may have been channeling what energy he had into marketing his own music, but there were problems with that, as well. After selling 205,000 copies of his new album, *Forever*, in the first week of its release, sales dropped; he sold just 119,000 copies the following week (according to *SoundScan*). Not only did the album not debut in the number-one spot, but by the third week it had fallen to number twenty-seven. Some members of the Puff Daddy camp claimed that Combs was distracted by Lopez.

Combs, however, maintained that he was on top of the situation, and the fun and games continued. On August 25, the *New York Post*'s "Page Six" gossip section reported that Combs had "interviewed" Jennifer Lopez for his magazine, *Notorious*. Among other things, Combs asked Lopez about the type of guy she likes ("a tough exterior, but sweet inside") and if she had any favorite sex aids ("handcuffs and/or whipped cream"). In a similar vein, *New York Daily News* gossip duo Rush and Molloy revealed that Jennifer had expressed a willingness to engage in a ménage à trois with a future husband, but only if the third partner was another woman, "so my husband could enjoy it."

Any lingering doubts that Jennifer and Sean were now officially together were dispelled by September. The *New York Daily News* reported on September 7 that at Puffy's annual White Party, held at his Easthampton estate, he and Lopez had held hands, danced together, and slipped away for some extended private moments in his bedroom. When they came up for air they were spotted on a balcony, where they kissed in full view of the assembled guests. "For a couple who are notoriously elusive about the state of their relationship, they left no doubt that they are very together," remarked one witness. The game of cat and mouse appeared to be over at last.

The question of what Lopez's next career move would be was also answered at about this time, when it was announced that she had signed a five-million-dollar deal to costar with Vince Vaughn, of *The Lost World* and *Swingers*, in a thriller called *The Cell*. It looked as though her recording career would flourish, as well: she received four MTV Video Music Award nominations for the "If You Had My Love" video.

Jennifer would be prominently featured at the televised awards ceremonies, but some of the recognition she received had little to do with respect for her music. During his opening monologue, host Chris Rock made Lopez the butt, so to speak, of some harsh jokes. "Jennifer Lopez here tonight, Jennifer Lopez. She came with two limos, one for her and one for her ass. I love Jennifer. Where you at girl? You don't thank your ass enough. I see Jennifer on TV thanking her momma and daddy and her acting coach. Thank your ass girl, thank your ass, before your ass goes solo, cause the ass is the star of the show. Jennifer is just the Commodores — her ass is Lionel Ritchie." Later that night Jennifer infuriated reporter Jorge Estevez of New

Accepting the Most Fashionable Artist-Female Award at the
VH1–Vogue Fashion Awards, 1999

AFP / CORBIS

York's News 12 the Bronx by backing out of a promised interview. Estevez retaliated by leading off his story with the item that Lopez had been shut out at the awards, losing in all four categories in which she had been nominated.

On December 5, at the fifth annual VH1/Vogue Fashion Awards in New York City — hosted by Heather Locklear and Puff Daddy — Lopez fared better, being voted Most Fashionable Female Artist. Her dress, a gold, cleavage-displaying Gucci gown by designer of the year Tom Ford, was also a hit. But Jennifer made it clear that to her wearing revealing clothes was a fashion, not a moral, statement. "People equate sexy with promiscuous," she said. "They think that because I'm shaped this way, I must be scandalous

— like running around and bringing men into my hotel room. But it's just the opposite."

Jennifer had always maintained that she was a one-man woman, and now, it appeared, Combs was ready to be a one-woman man. Rush and Molloy reported that at his November 1999 birthday bash Combs had told his friends, "I never had anyone love me the way she loves me. I love her and, hopefully, one day I will be able to marry her." Lopez wasn't there to hear these sweet words because she was in Los Angeles filming *The Cell*. She did, however, send Puffy videotaped birthday wishes in which she dressed up as Marilyn Monroe, complete with blond wig and tight dress, and sang "Happy Birthday" — just like Marilyn did for President Kennedy. Rumors then began circulating that Puffy and Jennifer were planning a New Year's Eve wedding in Miami.

In December 1999, *People* magazine included Lopez on its 25 Most Intriguing People of '99 list. The accompanying article reported that Jennifer's representatives denied the engagement. It also offered this insight from *Cell* producer Julio Caro: "[Jennifer's] just not someone who will do the obvious or logical choice. She's always pushing that envelope."

Rough Times and Good Instincts

It sometimes seems that Jennifer is genetically incapable of keeping a low profile. In November 1999, *People* ran an item about trouble on the set of her new film, *The Cell*, in which she plays a child psychologist who enters the mind of a comatose serial killer. The film includes several fantasy or dream sequences for which Lopez had to wear a number of wigs. *People*'s Tom Cunneff reported that the film's original hairdresser left the project soon after filming began. She claimed that she hadn't been allowed to speak directly to Jennifer and was required to communicate through inter-mediaries. Producer Julio Caro denied this, explaining that the hairdresser had left because her experience with wigs was insufficient. "There's a big difference between hair and wigs," Caro told Cunneff, adding, "Jennifer is quite accessible. She has an assistant on the set, but we all communicate directly with her."

It must have occasionally seemed to Jennifer that her assistant, Arlene, with whom she had been friends since grade school, was the only person she could trust. Even ex-husband Ojani Noa had let her down. He did a tell-all interview with the British tabloid *News of the World* for a hefty sum in which he described his dramatic escape from Cuba on a balsa-wood raft and claimed that Jennifer had picked him up while he was a waiter. He also said that having sex with her was like "bathing in champagne." The American tabloid *Globe* picked up where the *News* left off, running its own story under the screaming headline "Sex-Crazed Jennifer Lopez Dumped Me." "We did whatever two humans could possibly do," Noa reportedly said. "We'd make love in the kitchen while dinner was cooking" — when they were driving, he added, they'd sometimes pull off the road and hop into the backseat. It was Jennifer, he insisted, who proposed to him — and who wanted out of the marriage a few months later.

Shortly before Christmas 1999, the New York gossip columnists couldn't seem to make up their minds about Combs and Lopez. Were they planning on living happily ever after or on the verge of splitting up? Depending upon which newspaper you read and on what day, either Puffy was going to dump Jennifer because she was (according to Neal Travis of the *New York Post*) "a bit too assertive for his taste," or he was presenting her with a mink coat and an antique diamond bracelet (as reported by the *New York Daily News* duo of Rush and Molloy). Then there were the anonymous sources who claimed it was Jennifer who was trying to break away from Combs.

One thing was certain, however: on December 26, 1999, the two were very much together at Club New York on West 43rd Street in Manhattan. There a chain of events would occur, culminating in a shooting, that would land Jennifer in the midst of the biggest scandal of her life.

There are as many versions of what happened at Club New York that night as there are witnesses — and then some. But a scan of police and news reports yields this account. Puffy and Jennifer were at the club accompanied by one of Puffy's Bad Boy artists, Shyne, a nineteen-year-old rapper whose real name is Jamal Barrow; Puffy's bodyguard, Anthony "Wolf" Jones, considered by many of Puffy's friends to be the type of companion Combs should be removing from his life; and a group of about thirty friends. According to several eyewitnesses, Combs was flaunting his wealth by tossing wads of cash around — it was later determined that he was carrying about eight thousand dollars — to the annoyance of some of the club's other patrons. They eventually confronted him, and one man allegedly threw a stack of bills back at Combs.

It was alleged that Combs then brandished a gun. Normally anyone entering the club has to pass through metal detectors, but because Puffy was a VIP, neither he nor anyone with him was required to suffer the indignity of waiting in line or being scanned for weaponry. After Combs allegedly pulled out a gun, so did Shyne. The young rapper then opened fire with his 9mm Ruger. "Everybody hit the floor and people started screaming," reported a witness. "It was pandemonium." Three bystanders were hit — a woman was shot in the face and two men were struck in the shoulder —

although no one was fatally wounded. In the confusion and panic that immediately ensued, Combs and Lopez fled from the scene in his Lincoln Navigator suv, along with his driver and a bodyguard, an ex-convict who had once been imprisoned for shooting at a cop. According to the Manhattan prosecutor assigned to the case, Puffy and Jennifer attempted to evade the pursuing police, running at least ten red lights in the process. When officers finally succeeded in pulling their car over, they claimed to have discovered a stolen 9mm in the vehicle. Everyone was taken into custody.

Lopez was held for almost fourteen hours, reportedly handcuffed to a bench, and she spent the early-morning hours of December 27 weeping uncontrollably. But one of Puffy's lawyers, Ed Hayes, later denied that Jennifer had broken down. Speaking to *Talk* magazine's Bob Morris, Hayes said, "She's a capable person and despite what was in the tabloids she was not hysterical that night. When I was talking to her she had tremendous focus and charisma and if she appeared to be a mess, it was only as a way to manipulate the cops. Of course she cried, but that didn't mean she didn't have total control of the situation." As Jennifer got set to leave, Hayes continued, a large crowd of officers and detectives gathered to get a look at the movie star; when she walked away, "she gave them a little wiggle with her hips that made them smile. The woman is a giant." Hayes did admit, however, that Lopez was very concerned about how her mother would react to the situation, and at one point she commented, "My mother's going to be so upset."

In the end, she was cleared of any wrongdoing. Outside the precinct house, Jennifer's lawyer, Larry Ruggiero, made this statement to a crowd of reporters: "Jennifer Lopez, who was detained and questioned by police today at the 35th precinct in NYC, has been exonerated of all charges connected to the possession of an illegal firearm. Jennifer has been released. . . . Ms. Lopez was detained and questioned and fully cooperated with authorities. Jennifer Lopez does not own a firearm nor does she condone the use of firearms."

In court that morning for Combs's arraignment, the prosecutor admitted that the witnesses he'd lined up were willing to testify that they'd only seen Combs pull out a gun; nobody would say they actually saw him shoot it. Combs's attorney Harvey Slovis argued before the judge that it was not only false but also illogical to assert that his client was guilty of either brandishing a weapon or firing it. "Jennifer Lopez is a very famous actress,"

Lopez leaves court after testifying before the Grand Jury in New York, 1999
FRANCES M. ROBERTS / LIAISON AGENCY

Slovis said. "And to think Mr. Combs is walking with Miss Lopez with a loaded gun, and he is not the shooter, and then left. He goes to the car, and he still has the gun. It's ridiculous." The attorney also pointed out that the gun had been found in the front of the Navigator and that "it's not reasonable to charge the people in the back." Bail was finally set at ten thousand dollars, and Combs was freed.

If there was ever a time for Lopez to cut her losses and run as fast as she could away from Combs, it was now. Instead, she seemed more determined than ever to stand beside him. After their release she and Combs went back to their room at the Peninsula Hotel. There they prepared for the inevitable fallout. The next day, they met with Slovis and Puffy's publicist, Dan Klores, to work out what Combs would say at a scheduled press conference. According to *Talk*'s Michael Daly, it was Lopez who insisted, "the whole thing is, you had no gun." When the time came to face the press, Combs looked positively collegiate in an understated pullover sweater and slacks. He made his statement. "On Sunday evening, I went to Club New York. Under no circumstances whatsoever did I have anything to do with a shooting. I do not own a gun, nor did I possess a gun, that night. I want to make this one-hundred-percent clear. I had nothing to do with a shooting in this club, and I feel terrible that people were hurt that night. I'm positive, in the next couple of days, due to the investigation, that the truth will come out."

Eventually, Combs would be indicted and charged with criminal possession of a weapon and criminal possession of stolen property; the pistol allegedly found in the Navigator had been reported stolen in August from a pickup truck in suburban Atlanta. Officials at the Bureau of Alcohol, Tobacco and Firearms and the New York police said that the 9mm Smith & Wesson model 915 was the same one reported stolen by a construction worker named Ralph Cooper, of Powder Springs, Cobb County, Georgia. "He hadn't seen the gun for about a month and then reported it missing. A cell phone was also taken from the truck," Powder Springs police Sergeant Matt Atkins explained. The case is still pending, but if convicted Combs faces up to fifteen months in jail.

Combs's bodyguard, Anthony "Wolf" Jones, and the driver of the Navigator, Wardel Fenderson, also face weapons charges. Shyne faces three counts of attempted murder. Fenderson has deepened his former employer's legal woes by telling police that Puffy tried to bribe him to say that the gun found in the Navigator was his. Dan Klores, however, vehemently denies it. The gun did not belong to Combs, he says; his client is "a mere victim of circumstance" who was "fleeing a life-threatening situation."

But from the moment the story broke Puffy's notoriety has been intensifying. He has become a marked man. Articles have appeared rehashing his past violent encounters and less savory activities. It's been said that when he was a student at Howard University he earned extra cash by selling term papers and old exams. A report surfaced that a photographer, Donnell Mitchell, who said he had been hired by Arista Records to shoot Combs and Lopez at a radio promotion in Cleveland, was attacked by Puffy's bodyguard, who then stole his film. Mitchell charged that after he snapped Lopez a security goon grabbed him by the shirt and threw him against a car several times. It was also widely reported that Puffy could have been sentenced to seven years in prison — instead of one day in an anger-management course — for attacking Interscope's Stoute if Stoute hadn't agreed to lesser charges after Combs paid him half a million dollars.

Yet Puffy has never acted to protect himself by choosing his companions more carefully. Why he would insist on hanging out with the likes of Shyne and Wolf remains a puzzle. Some say Puffy thought he needed the kind of protection a man like Wolf could offer because of the hostility Suge Knight felt for him and the fact that Notorious B.I.G.'s killer has never been identified. His connection to Shyne is less clear; the would-be rapper sensation was obviously trouble just waiting to happen. Shortly after signing with Bad Boy, Shyne crashed his new Mercedes, and the accident resulted in the death of a friend. Then, just a few months before the club shooting, Shyne was involved in a fight; afterwards, an unidentified individual shot at him in Puffy's recording studio. "Puffy has to address issues of personal growth and change," Klores told *Newsweek*. "Then you can begin to address the matter of people's perception of him."

As Puffy's life was being dissected, so was Jennifer's — but in her case the media generally stuck to the theme of "What's a nice girl like this doing with a bad guy like that?" According to *Newsweek*'s Johnnie L. Roberts and Allison Samuels, Lopez was under a lot of pressure to separate herself from Combs even before the shooting. A close friend of Jennifer's was quoted as saying, "The people around her were worried that something like this would happen. They have repeatedly told her that you can't be Hollywood's sweetheart if you're running from the cops." Another anonymous source told Tom Sinclair of *Entertainment Weekly*, "She's old enough to know better. Everyone should make a New Year's wish for her that she finds a new boyfriend."

Of course it's not so simple. As yet another friend of Jennifer's put it, "It's tough for her because she does really love Puffy. He has what she likes — determination and aggressiveness. But she also knows it might be a choice between a doomed relationship and a doomed career."

Jennifer herself says, "I fire up very easily. I like excitement. I don't drink or do drugs or even smoke, but I'm still the one who will get up on a table and dance. . . . I definitely have a wild side." She also longs to remarry, settle down, and have children. She has a very strong sense of family, which is why buying a Los Angeles home was so symbolic for her. "Family to me is everything — there is nothing else," she said on a March 2000 MTV special. "Everything else goes away. There's only one place you go — home." She went on to say that she always takes comfort in the understanding

Lopez and Puffy at the 2000 Grammy Awards

that "no matter what else happens, knowing that my whole family could live in the house the rest of our lives is the best feeling in the world."

To those who had been implying that she was just a Puffy puppet, Jennifer had this to say: "The bottom line is, I'm where I am because I want to be. Nobody really forces me to do anything. That could be one of the best things about me and it could be one of the worst, I don't know." She added that she was learning the importance of being alone — because that's when "you get to listen to *you*, to the voices in your head. I think that's what we avoid a lot of times because it's usually the truth and the truth is hard to deal with." Jennifer's way of dealing with what has befallen her and Puffy is to keep moving forward, even though the charges hanging over Combs's head are "scary. It's not something we dwell on. It'll be a happy day once it's not something we have to think about."

Another way Jennifer copes is, of course, by immersing herself in her work. After wrapping *The Cell*, she started filming a romantic comedy called *The Wedding Planner*, opposite Matthew McConaughey. She's described the experience as the most fun she's ever had on a movie set. Lopez also busied herself by making more fashion headlines at the 2000 Grammys. Her Versace palm-print silk chiffon dress somehow managed to make her look more naked than she'd be if she had worn nothing at all. Lopez maintains that she had no idea — really — that the gown would cause such a media stir. "I thought it was a beautiful dress," she protested, then laughed. "When I came out [to present an award] they were all shocked and appalled." Her copresenter, *X-Files* star David Duchovny, quipped, "Jennifer, this is the first time in five or six years I'm *sure* nobody is looking at *me*." After Lopez left the stage, Rosie O'Donnell, who hosted the ceremonies, meowed, "It's nice to see Jennifer in a classy little understated number like that. And she wonders why people make fun of her body." Actually, few members of the audience appeared to be making fun. But there were plenty of dropped jaws.

For days afterwards, newspapers and television entertainment shows ran photos of Lopez in that sheer, cut-to-the-navel dress. Everyone was asking, "How did she keep it from falling open and revealing all?" In a March 6 *Entertainment Tonight* segment, Lopez supplied the answer. Toupee tape. "It wasn't going to move," she said. "It didn't seem that out there to me. It was a good-looking dress. It wasn't as open as it looked on TV. I had no idea it was going to be such a big deal."

In late March, Lopez appeared on *Access Hollywood* and talked about her relationship with Combs without ever once saying his name. She admitted that they had been going through some rough times, but she seemed determined to move forward. "We're not through it yet. Hopefully, everything will come out okay. We have each other. There are ups and downs. You make the best of it." As for the future, "I do want to have kids and I do want to get married," she said. "Who knows if it will be anytime soon." Lopez has also described herself as "very romantic. I believe that if I haven't found Prince Charming already that I will; or he will find me, if he hasn't already."

But Jennifer's dream of love and domestic harmony is still being stalled by the harsh realities facing Combs. Adding to an already-tense situation was the news, which was issued in late February, that Puffy had been indicted yet again, this time on that Fenderson bribery charge: Puffy and Wolf Jones were charged with offering Fenderson fifty thousand dollars in cash and a diamond ring — a birthday present given to Combs by Lopez — to say that he owned the gun found in the Navigator. "I am outraged by this new charge," Combs said in a statement. "I am not guilty. From the outset I have firmly believed that the Manhattan district attorney's office has unfairly targeted me for baseless charges." The bribery charge carries a penalty of seven years in prison.

Jennifer has continued to stand by Puffy, and so far she has experienced little if any professional fallout. Her L'Oreal spokesperson deal remains intact, the movie roles keep coming, and she's proceeding with plans for a new album. As far as her personal life goes, she looks to the future and tries to follow her heart. "I really trust myself; I trust my instincts," she said during her MTV *Diary* appearance. "My heart is the ruler of all my being — who I am, where I want to be, who I want to be with. If my heart tells me it's true and right, then that's good enough for me."

Sources

CHAPTER 1
Brantley Bardin, *Details*, qtd. in Denis Ferrara and Diane Judge, "Puff Daddy's Pal?" *Newsday* 22 Nov. 1998; Dennis Duggan, "A Rising Latina Star Wows Them in Bronx," *Newsday* 20 Mar. 1997; Michael A. Gonzales, *Latina* Mar. 1999; David Handleman, *Mirabella* Aug. 1998; Julian Ives, *Mr. Showbiz* 1997; Anthony Noguera, *FHM* 1998; Martyn Palmer, *Total Film* Dec. 1998.

CHAPTER 2
"Glued to the Tube: Comedy, Drama — Get It?" *Newsday* 5 Apr. 1994; David Handleman, *Mirabella* Aug. 1998; David Hiltbrand, "Picks & Pans: Tube," *People* 20 Dec. 1993, and 8 Aug. 1994; Neal Justin, "The Wonderful World of 'Color,'" *Minneapolis-Star Tribune* 26 Aug. 1997; Marvin Kitman, "The Marvin Kitman Show: Take In 'Second Chances,'" *Newsday* 2 Dec. 1993; Bob Morris, "Line of Fire," *Talk* Mar. 2000; Clarence Page, "Networks Tune Out Black Americans," *St. Louis Post-Dispatch* 9 June 1994; Gail Pennington, "'Hotel Malibu' Checks In," *St. Louis Post-Dispatch* 4 Aug. 1994, and "'Seinfeld' West Has Its Fun with . . . Whatever," *St. Louis Post-Dispatch* 27 Mar. 1994; Ray Richmond, "'South Central' Criticized as Depicting Stereotypes," *St. Louis Post-Dispatch* 5 May 1994; Kyle Smith, et al, "Shaking It Up," *People* 13 Sept. 1999; Bob Thomas, "Connie and John: Lessons in Love," *Good Housekeeping* Mar. 1994; Ken Tucker, "'After the Lovin': Connie Sellecca Blows Off an Old Flame," *Entertainment Weekly* 3 Dec. 1993, and "Summer's Resorts," *Entertainment Weekly* 5 Aug. 1994.

CHAPTER 3
Gregory Freeman, "TV Can Change the Channel on Hispanic Roles," *St. Louis Post-Dispatch* 9 Dec. 1994; Mike Hughes, "TV or Not TV," *Gannett News Service* 1 Aug. 1994; Caryn James, "'My Family' a Warmhearted, Ambitious, Uneven Story," *Minneapolis Star-Tribune* 19 May 1995; Kirby Tepper, "My Family/Mi Familia," *Magill's Survey of Cinema* 15 June 1995; Dennis West, "Filming the Chicano Family Saga," *Cineaste* 1 Dec. 1995.

CHAPTER 4
Tom Green, "'Money' Cashes In on Stars' Friendly Rivalry," *USA Today* 22 Nov. 1995; Stephen Rebello, *Movieline* Feb. 1998.

CHAPTER 5

John Anderson, "'Money Train' Is Right on Time," *Newsday* 22 Nov. 1995; Carolyn Bingham, "'Money Train': Wesley Runs Away with It," *Los Angeles Sentinel* 22 Nov. 1995; Mark Harris, ed., *Entertainment Weekly* Fall Movie Preview 25 Aug. 1995; Hillary Johnson, "Beauty Talk," *In Style* Apr. 1997; "On the Rise: Feeling the Heat, 'Money Train's' Jennifer Lopez Worries about Copycat Pyros,"*People* 11 Dec. 1995; Stephen Rebello, *Movieline* Feb. 1998; "Scene & Heard, News to Amuse: A Star-Studded Review," *In Style* Nov. 1995; Kyle Smith, et al, "Shaking It Up . . . ," *People* 13 Sept. 1999; Jeff Strickler, "'Money Train' Arrives Late, Then Delivers," *Minneapolis Star-Tribune* 22 Nov. 1999.

CHAPTER 6

John Anderson, "A Stew of Lust, Diamonds, and Contempt," *Newsday* 21 Feb. 1997; Robert Denerstein, "Taste of 'Blood and Wine' Is a Bitter One," *Rocky Mountain News* 14 Mar. 1997; Howard Feinstein, "Bob and Jack's Excellent Adventures," *Newsday* 2 Feb. 1997; Nick Hasted, "The Man Who Invented Jack Nicholson," *Independent* 10 Mar. 1997; Dennis Hensley, "How Do You Say 'Hot' in Spanish?" *Cosmopolitan* Apr. 1997; John Simon, "Tin Cup," *National Review* 16 Sept. 1996; Elizabeth Llorente, "Her Latina Self," *Record* 21 July 1996; Jack Matthews, "Boy, 10, Doomed to Be Robin Williams," *Newsday* 9 Aug. 1996; Anita McDivitt, "New Women's Magazine Uses a Different Tone," *Dallas Morning News* 26 June 1996; Kevin Newman, "Jennifer Lopez, Tough Cop," *Good Morning America* [ABC] 6 July 1998; Matt Roush, *USA Today* 9 Aug. 1996; Chris Vognar, "'Blood and Wine' Isn't Vintage Stuff," *Dallas Morning News* 14 Mar. 1997; James M. Welsh, "Jack," *Magill's Survey of Cinema* 21 Sept. 1996.

CHAPTER 7

Mike Clark, "'Anaconda' Has Surprising Grip," *USA Today* 10 Oct. 1997; "The Crime: Fatal Attraction Fired by the Singer She Adored," *People* 5 May 1995; Jack Garner, "The Worst Thing to Happen to a Snake . . . ," *Gannett News Service* 8 Apr. 1997; S.C. Gwynne, "Death of a Rising Star," *Time* 10 Apr. 1995; Dennis Hensley, "How Do You Say 'Hot' In Spanish?" *Cosmopolitan* Apr. 1997; Bill Hewitt, et al, "Up Front: Before Her Time Touted as Latin Music's Madonna," *People* 17 Apr. 1995; Adina Hoffman, "The Serpent's Tale Lacks Bite," *Jerusalem Post* 29 Aug. 1997; Lisa Schwarzbaum, "This Mortal Coil: 'Anaconda' Squeezes Out Some Big B-Movie Moments," *Entertainment Weekly* 18 Apr. 1997; Robert Seidenberg, "Legacy Requiem for a Latin Star," *Entertainment Weekly* 14 Apr. 1995; Patrick Stoner, *Flicks* Apr. 1997.

CHAPTER 8

Henri Béhar, *Film Scouts*; Hillary Johnson, "Beauty Talk," *In Style* Apr. 1997; Luaine Lee, "Olmos Cleared a Path for Hispanics," *Minneapolis Star-Tribune* 17 May 1997;

Jeffrey Ressner, "Born to Play the Tejano Queen," *Time International* 24 Mar. 1997; Mario Tarradell, "Selena's Power: Cultural Fusion," *Dallas Morning News* 16 Mar. 1997; Cynthia L. Webb, "Hispanic Films still Looking for Audience," *Rocky Mountain News* 30 Nov. 1997; Bruce Westbrook, "'Selena' Actress Is on Star Track," *Dallas Morning News* 2 Aug. 1996.

CHAPTER 9

James Berardinelli, film.com 1997; Richard Corliss, "¡Viva Selena!" *Time* 24 Mar. 1997; Roger Ebert, "Lopez a Convincing Selena," *Minneapolis Star-Tribune* 21 Mar. 1997; Lynn Elber, "'Selena' Gives a Boost to Hispanics in Films," *Dallas Morning News* 20 Apr. 1997; Eric Guitierrez, "Busting Boundaries," *Newsday* 16 Mar. 1997; Jack Matthews, "Though Muted by Dad, 'Selena' Sings," *Newsday* 21 Mar. 1997; Jeffrey Ressner, "Born to Play the Tejano Queen," *Time International* 24 Mar. 1997; Virginia Rohan, "The Spirit of Selena," *Record* 20 Mar. 1997; Lisa Schwarzbaum, "You've Heard the Song Before," *Entertainment Weekly* 28 Mar. 1997; Paul Souhrada, "Putting on the Glitz," *Dallas Morning News* 29 Mar. 1997; Mario Tarradell, "Selena's Power: Cultural Fusion," *Dallas Morning News* 16 Mar. 1997; Karen Thomas, "Two Stories of Selena Movie," *usa Today* 4 Mar. 1997; Mimi Valdes, "Butter Pecan Rican," *Vibe* June/July 1997; Chris Vognar, "'Selena': Biopic Set Firmly in Ode Mode," *Dallas Morning News* 21 Mar. 1997; Cynthia L. Webb, "Hispanic Films still Looking for Audience," *Rocky Mountain News* 30 Nov. 1997.

CHAPTER 10

Dennis Duggan, "A Rising Latina Star Wows Them in Bronx," *Newsday* 20 Mar. 1997; Marha Frankel, "Love in Bloom," *In Style* Feb. 1998; Dennis Hensley, "How Do You Say 'Hot' in Spanish?" *Cosmopolitan* Apr. 1997; Janet Maslin, *New York Times* 4 June 1998; Bob Morris, "Line of Fire," *Talk* Mar. 2000; Yaak Ngern-maak, "Take Five: Films That Will Twist Your Mind and Make You Think," *Nation* [Thailand] 4 June 1998; Anthony Noguera, FHM 1998; Penny Proddow, et al, "Heart and Soul Classics," *In Style* Feb. 1998; Stephen Rebello, *Movieline* 1998; Jeffrey Ressner, "Born to Play the Tejano Queen," *Time International* 24 Mar. 1997; Gene Seymour, "New Paths for Oliver Stone," *Newsday* 5 Oct. 1997; Kyle Smith, et al, "Shaking It Up," *People* 13 Sept. 1999.

CHAPTER 11

Colin Covert, "'Out of Sight' Is One Worth Seeing," *Minneapolis Star-Tribune* 26 June 1998; Owen Gleiberman, "It Takes a Thief," *Entertainment Weekly* 26 June 1998; Sarah Gristwood, "Steamy and Sexy," *Edmonton Sun* 22 Nov. 1998; Janet Maslin, *New York Times* 26 June 1998; Margaret A. McGurk, "This Role Clooney Really Wanted," *Gannett News Service* 30 June 1998; "Names in the News," AP Online 22 June 1998; "1998: The Year That Was . . . Memorable Moments from Stage and Screen," *Entertainment Weekly* 25 Dec. 1998; John Powers and Terry

Gross, "Out of Sight," *Fresh Air*, National Public Radio 10 July 1998; Stephen Schaefer, "Plenty of Clooney in View in 'Out of Sight' Love Scene," *USA Today* 12 June 1998; Jeannie Williams, "Jennifer Lopez: She's Proud of Her Bottom Line," *USA Today* 2 July 1998; Philip Wuntch, "Clooney Tunes Up His Career with New Film," *Dallas Morning News* 26 June 1998.

CHAPTER 12

Cindy Adams, "Cindy's Romantic Dish," *Good Morning America* 12 June 1998; Brantley Bardin, *Details*, qtd. in Denis Ferrara and Diane Judge, "Puff Daddy's Pal?" *Newsday* 22 Nov. 1998; Editorial Staff, *In Style* June 1999; Denis Ferrara and Diane Judge, "Puff Daddy's Pal?" *Newsday* 22 Nov. 1998; "The 50 Most Beautiful People in the World," *People* 12 May 1997; Angelo Figueroa, *Face of Journalism*, National Public Radio 24 June 1998; Jeremy Helligar and Stephen Cojocaru, "Party: Acting Up More Outrageous . . . ," *People* 15 June 1998; Robert La Franco, "The Huff behind the Puff," *Forbes* 21 Sept. 1998; "Mailbag," *People* 21 Dec. 1998; Bob Morris, "Line of Fire," *Talk* Mar. 2000; "Names in the News," AP Online 14 Nov. 1998; Kevin Newman, "Jennifer Lopez, Tough Cop," *Good Morning America* 6 July 1998; "Page Six," *New York Post* 28 May 1998; Degen Pener, "Hey, Nude! Hollywood's Fashion Statement," *Style* June 1998, and "From Here to Divanity," *Entertainment Weekly* 9 Oct. 1998; Stephen Rebello, *Movieline* Feb. 1998; Sophronia Scott Gregory, et al, "On the Move: The Right Puff," *People* 18 Oct. 1998; Gene Seymour, "Acting Animated," *Newsday* 13 Dec. 1998; Kyle Smith, et al, "Shaking It Up," *People* 13 Sept. 1999; Stephanie Tuck, "Puff and Stuff: He Came, He Saw, He Redecorated," *In Style* Oct 1999.

CHAPTER 13

David Browne, *Entertainment Weekly* 4 June 1999; Veronica Chambers and John Leland, "Lovin' La Vida Loca," *Newsweek* 31 May 1999; Betty Cortina, "The Other Chili Peppers," *Entertainment Weekly* 9 July 1999; Daniel Durchholz, *Wall of Sound* June 1999; Editorial Staff, *In Style* June 1999; Christopher John Farley, "Latin Music Pops: We've Seen the Future," *Time* 24 May 1999; "The 50 Most Beautiful People in the World," *People* 10 May 1999; Dream Hampton, *Vibe* Aug. 1999; Louis B. Hobson, "Latino Actors still Fighting for Respect," *London Free Press* 8 July 1999; "Item," *New York Post* 25 Aug. 1999; "Page Six," *New York Post* 11 Sept. 1999; Johnnie L. Roberts, "Puffy's Crowded Orbit," *Newsweek* 8 Nov. 1999; Rush and Molloy, *New York Daily News* 27 May 1999, 25 Aug. 1999, 7 Sept. 1999, and 7 Nov. 1999; Corey Takahashi, "Latin Lovers Following in Ricky Martin's Dance Steps," *Entertainment Weekly* 19 Nov. 1999; Kathleen Tracy, *Ricky Martin: Red Hot and on the Rise*, Kensington 1999; "The 25 Most Intriguing People of '99," *People* 31 Dec. 1999; Mike Usinger, *Infoculture* [www.infoculture.com]; Ben Wener, *Orange County Register* 29 May 1999.

CHAPTER 14

Access Hollywood 21 Mar. 2000; Patrice Baldwin, "Sex-Crazed Jennifer Lopez Dumped Me! After Only 15 Months, Says Ex-Hubby," *Globe* 4 Jan. 2000; Tom Cunneff, "Insider," *People* 1 Nov. 1999; Michael Daly, *Talk* Mar. 2000; *Entertainment Tonight* 6 Mar. 2000; Bob Morris, "Line of Fire," *Talk* Mar. 2000; *MTV Diary* 29 Mar. 2000; Johnnie L. Roberts and Allison Samuels, *Newsweek* 10 Jan. 2000; Rush and Molloy, *New York Daily News* 24 Dec. 1999; Tom Sinclair, "Daddy Oh!" *Entertainment Weekly* 7 Jan. 2000; Neal Travis, *New York Post* 20 Dec. 2000.